Teacher...
Inspire...
Lead...

MW00415089

Research & Education Association

The Best Teachers' Test Preparation for the

FTCE
English 6–12

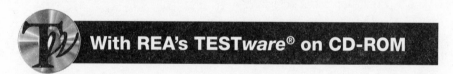

With REA's TEST*ware®* on CD-ROM

Alicia Mendoza, Ed.D.
Florida International University
Miami, Florida

Visit our Educator Support Center at:
www.REA.com/teacher

The competencies presented in this book were created and implemented by the Florida Department of Education in conjunction with National Evaluation Systems, Inc. For further information visit the FTCE website at *www.fldoe.org/asp/ftce.*

Research & Education Association
61 Ethel Road West
Piscataway, New Jersey 08854
E-mail: info@rea.com

**The Best Teachers' Test Preparation for the
FTCE English 6–12 Test
With TEST*ware*® on CD-ROM**

Printed in the United States of America

Library of Congress Control Number 2008928188

ISBN-13: 978-0-7386-0458-9
ISBN-10: 0-7386-0458-5

Windows® is a registered trademark of Microsoft Corporation.

F08-0101

About Research & Education Association

Founded in 1959, Research & Education Association is dedicated to publishing the finest and most effective educational materials—including software, study guides, and test preps—for students in middle school, high school, college, graduate school, and beyond.

REA's Test Preparation series includes books and software for all academic levels in almost all disciplines. Research & Education Association publishes test preps for students who have not yet entered high school, as well as for high school students preparing to enter college. Students from countries around the world seeking to attend college in the United States will find the assistance they need in REA's publications. For college students seeking advanced degrees, REA publishes test preps for many major graduate school admission examinations in a wide variety of disciplines, including engineering, law, and medicine. Students at every level, in every field, with every ambition can find what they are looking for among REA's publications.

REA's practice tests are always based upon the most recently administered exams and include every type of question that you can expect on the actual exams.

REA's publications and educational materials are highly regarded and continually receive an unprecedented amount of praise from professionals, instructors, librarians, parents, and students. Our authors are as diverse as the fields represented in the books we publish. They are well-known in their respective disciplines and serve on the faculties of prestigious high schools, colleges, and universities throughout the United States and Canada.

Today, REA's wide-ranging catalog is a leading resource for teachers, students, and professionals.

We invite you to visit us at *www.rea.com* to find out how REA is making the world smarter.

Acknowledgments

We would like to thank Larry Kling, Vice President, Editorial, for his editorial direction; John Cording, Vice President, Technology, for coordinating the design, development, and testing of REA's TEST*ware*® software; Pam Weston, Vice President, Publishing, for setting the quality standards for production integrity and managing the publication to completion; Alice Leonard, Senior Editor, for project management and preflight editorial review; Diane Goldschmidt, Senior Editor, for post-production quality assurance; Amy Jamison, Technology Project Manager, for software testing; Christine Saul, Senior Graphic Artist, for cover design; Rachel DiMatteo, Graphic Artist, for test design; and Jeff LoBalbo, Senior Graphic Artist, for post-production file mapping.

We also gratefully acknowledge Barbara McGowran for copyediting, Kathy Caratozzolo of Caragraphics for typesetting, Ellen Gong for proofreading, and Stephanie Reymann for indexing the manuscript.

About the Author

Alicia Mendoza, Ed.D., formerly chair of the Elementary Education Department at Florida International University, has held the position of Associate Professor at the same academic institution for more than 31 years. Before coming to FIU, she was an Associate Professor at Clarion State College in Clarion, Pennsylvania, and served as a consultant to Head Start classes in Western Pennsylvania. She also taught in the public schools of New York City. She earned her Ed.D. and M.Ed. at the University of Miami, and her B.A. at Queens College in New York City. Dr. Mendoza has been the recipient of the Distinguished Member Award of the Association of Teacher Educators in 2005, a Teaching Incentive award, and an Excellence in Advising award during her time at Florida International University. She is the author of numerous published articles, book chapters, and curriculum materials. Dr. Mendoza also recently authored a book, *The Essentials of Elementary Education and Current Controversies*, and is a co-editor of REA's *The Best Teachers' Test Preparation for the FTCE General Knowledge Test*.

Contents

Introduction

ABOUT THIS BOOK AND TEST*ware*®

REA's *The Best Teachers' Test Preparation for the FTCE English 6–12 Test* is a comprehensive guide designed to assist you in preparing to take the FTCE, which is required in Florida to teach English in grades 6–12. To enhance your chances of success in this important step toward your career as a teacher in Florida schools, this test guide along with REA's exclusive TEST*ware*®, features:

- An accurate and complete overview of the FTCE English 6–12

- The information you need to know about the exam

- A targeted review of every competency and skill

- Tips and strategies for successfully completing standardized tests

- Diagnostic tools to identify areas of strength and weakness

- Two full-length, true-to-format practice tests based on the most recently administered FTCE English 6–12

- Detailed explanations for each question on the practice tests, enabling you to identify correct answers and understand not only why they are correct but also why the other answer choices are incorrect

This guide is the result of studying many resources. The editors considered the most recent test administrations and professional standards. They also researched information from the Florida Department of Education, professional journals, textbooks, and educators. The result is the best test preparation materials based on the latest information available.

Practice Tests 1 and 2 are both included in two formats: in printed form in this book and in TEST*ware*® format on the enclosed CD. We recommend that you begin your preparation by first taking the computerized version of the test. The software provides the added benefits of enforced timed conditions and instantaneous, accurate scoring, making it easier to pinpoint your strengths and weaknesses.

ABOUT THE FTCE ENGLISH 6–12 TEST

What Does the Test Cover?

The following table lists the competencies used as the basis for the FTCE English 6–12 and the approximate percentage of the total test that each competency entails. These competencies represent the knowledge that teams of teachers, subject area specialists, and district-level educators have determined to be important for beginning teachers. A thorough review of all the competencies, as well as the specific skills that demonstrate each, is the focus of this book.

Competencies and Percentages of Total Test Items

Competency	%
1. Knowledge of the English language and methods for effective teaching	20
2. Knowledge of writing and methods for effective teaching	20
3. Knowledge of the use of the reading process to construct meaning from a wide range of selections	20
4. Knowledge of literature and methods for effective teaching	20
5. Knowledge of listening, viewing, and speaking as methods for acquiring critical literacy	15
6. Knowledge of the methods for integration of the language arts	5
7. Ability to write well on a selection from poetry or prose, including fiction or nonfiction	*
* The writing section comprises 30 percent of the score for this subject area test.	

How Is the FTCE English 6–12 Scored?

The FTCE English 6–12 is a pass or fail test. Scores for the FTCE English 6–12 Test aggregate the multiple-choice questions score and the performance (essay) score based on these weightings: 70% multiple-choice, 30% essay. The exact number of multiple-choice questions you will need to correctly answer to pass the test will depend upon how well you do on the essay and, in truth, on which of the several forms of the test you are administered. However, for all practical purposes, you'll want to consider 70%, or 60 questions, as your benchmark. Be aware, however, that, according to the Florida Department of Education, on examinations like the FTCE English 6–12 which include written or oral performance components, "percentages are not provided because scoring these examinations involves a more complex process to arrive at 'combination scores' or 'part scores.' One result of this is that on performance-based examinations, several different combinations of multiple-choice and performance test scores may result in the same passing scale score of 200 for the FTCE."

When Will I Receive My Score Report, and What Will It Look Like?

Approximately one month after you take the test, your score report will be mailed to you. Your scores will be submitted electronically to the Bureau of Educator Certification. A copy of your score report is sent to the one Florida college or university and the one Florida school district that you indicate on your registration application.

When you receive your score report and have passed, only the word *Pass* will be reported. If you do not pass, you will receive a numeric score and will have to retake the test.

Can I Retake the Test?

If you do not achieve a passing grade on the FTCE English 6–12, don't panic. You can take the test again after 31 days, and during that time you can work seriously on improving your score. A score that does not match your expectations does not mean you should change your plans about teaching.

Who Administers the Test?

The Florida Department of Education develops the FTCE English 6–12. Subject area knowledge tested on the examination was identified and validated by committees of content specialists from Florida. Most committee members are public school teachers, but the committees also included district supervisors and college faculty. Selection of committee members is based on recommendations by professional associations, experts, and teachers' unions. Development of the appropriate content and difficulty levels of the exam involved literature reviews, teacher interviews, field-testing, and professional judgments. Testing services, including test administrations, for the FTCE are provided by National Evaluation Systems, Inc.

When Should I Take the Test?

Florida law requires that teachers demonstrate mastery of basic skills, professional knowledge, and the content area in which they are specializing. If you have graduated from a Florida state-approved teacher preparation program and made the decision to teach English in grades 6–12, you need to begin the process by applying for a Florida Temporary Certificate in that subject. The Bureau of Educator Certification will only evaluate your eligibility in the subjects you request on your application form. The Temporary Certificate is valid for three school years, allowing you time to complete the certification tests while teaching full time.

For high school graduates and out-of-state educators, the Bureau of Educator Certification will provide you with official information about which test(s) to take to complete the requirements for the professional certificate. The FTCE is usually administered four times a year in several locations throughout Florida. The usual testing day is Saturday, but the test may be taken on an alternate day if a conflict exists, such as a religious obligation. Special accommodations can also be made for applicants who are visually impaired, hearing impaired, physically disabled, or specific-learning disabled.

To receive information on upcoming administrations of the FTCE, consult the FTCE Registration Bulletin, which you can obtain by contacting:

Florida Department of Education
325 West Gaines Street, Suite 414
Tallahassee, FL 32399-0400
Phone: (413) 256-2893
Web site: *www.fldoe.org/asp/ftce*
Bureau of Educator Certification: *www.fldoe.org/edcert/*

The FTCE Registration Bulletin also includes information regarding test retakes and score reports.

Do I Pay a Registration Fee?

To take the FTCE, you must pay a registration fee. You can pay by personal check, money order, cashier's check, or credit card (Visa or MasterCard). Cash is not accepted. Contact the Florida Department of Education (see the information above) if you have questions about registration or any other aspect of the FTCE.

HOW TO USE THIS BOOK AND TESTware®

When Should I Start Studying?

It is never too early to start studying for the FTCE. The earlier you begin, the more time you will have to sharpen your skills. Do not procrastinate! Cramming is not an effective way to study because it does not allow you the time you need to think about the content, review the competencies, and take the practice tests. However, you should review the material one last time the night before the test administration.

What Do the Review Sections Cover?

The targeted review in this book is designed to help you sharpen the basic skills you need to approach the FTCE English 6–12, as well as provide strategies for attacking the questions.

Each teaching competency included in the FTCE is examined in a separate chapter. The skills required for all seven competencies are extensively discussed to optimize your understanding of what the examination covers.

Your schooling has taught you most of the information you need to answer the questions on the test. The education classes you took should have provided you with the know-how to make important decisions about situations you will face as a teacher. The review sections in this book are designed to help you fit the information you have acquired into the competencies specified on the FTCE. Going over your class notes and textbooks together with the competency reviews provided here will give you an excellent springboard for passing the examination.

STUDYING FOR THE FTCE ENGLISH 6–12 TEST

Choose the time and place for studying that works best for you. Some people set aside a certain number of hours every morning to study, while others prefer to study at night before going to sleep. Other people study off and on during the day—for instance, while waiting for a bus or during a lunch break. Only you can determine when and where your study time will be most effective. Be consistent and use your time efficiently. Work out a study routine and stick to it.

When you take the practice tests, simulate the conditions of the actual test as closely as possible. Turn off your television and radio, and sit down at a table in a quiet room, free from distraction. On completing a practice test, score it and thoroughly review the explanations to the questions you answered incorrectly; however, do not review too much at any one time. Concentrate on one problem area at a time by reviewing the question and explanation, and by studying the review in this guide until you are confident that you have mastered the material.

Keep track of your scores so you can gauge your progress and discover general weaknesses in particular sections. Give extra attention to the reviews that cover your areas of difficulty, thus building your skills in those areas.

How Can I Use My Study Time Efficiently?

The following study schedule allows for thorough preparation for the FTCE English 6–12. The course of study presented here is seven weeks, but you can condense or expand the timeline to suit your personal schedule. It is vital that you adhere to a structured plan and set aside ample time each day to study. The more time you devote to studying, the more prepared and confident you will be on the day of the test.

STUDY SCHEDULE

Week 1	After having read this first chapter to understand the format and content of this exam, take the first TEST*ware*® practice test on CD. The score will indicate your strengths and weaknesses. Make sure you simulate real exam conditions when you take the test. Review the explanations, especially for questions you answered incorrectly.
Week 2	Review the appropriate chapter sections for material you missed. Useful study techniques include highlighting key terms and information, taking notes as you review each section, and putting new terms and information on note cards to help retain the information.
Weeks 3 and 4	Reread all your note cards, refresh your understanding of the competencies and skills included in the exam, review your college textbooks, and read over notes you took in your college classes. This is also the time to consider any other supplementary materials that your counselor or the Florida Department of Education suggests. Review the department's Web site at *www.fldoe.org*.
Week 5	Begin to condense your notes and findings. A structured list of important facts and concepts, based on your note cards and the FTCE English 6–12 competencies, will help you thoroughly review for the test. Review the answers and explanations for any questions you missed.
Week 6	Have someone quiz you using the note cards you created. Take the second practice test on CD-ROM, adhering to the time limits, which will be automatically incorporated in the TEST*ware*® program. Be sure to otherwise simulate test day conditions.
Week 7	Using all your study materials, review areas of weakness revealed by your score on the practice test. Then retake one or both of the practice tests in this book.

FORMAT OF THE FTCE ENGLISH 6–12 TEST

What Types of Questions Are on the Test?

The FTCE English 6–12 addresses seven main areas of competency identified by the Florida Department of Education as foundational to effective teaching. Within the seven competencies are 42 skill areas on which you will be questioned to assess your mastery of

English as taught in grades 6–12. Individual test items require a variety of different thinking levels, ranging from simple recall to evaluation and problem solving.

The competencies are broad statements written in a way to reflect the information that an entry-level educator needs to be an effective teacher. Only the skills will be discussed on the actual FTCE.

The FTCE English 6–12 consists of two parts: an essay and approximately 85 multiple-choice questions. You will have one hour to complete the essay and one-and-one-half hours to answer the multiple-choice questions. Each multiple-choice question has four answer choices, lettered A through D, from which to select the one correct answer.

For the essay, you will choose between two topics. This section represents 30 percent of your total score of the exam. Your essay will be scored by two judges on substance and on the composition skills demonstrated, including the following elements: ideas, focus, organization, style (diction and sentence structure), and mechanics (capitalization, punctuation, spelling, and usage). More information on the essay section is available in Chapter 8 of this review and on the website of the Florida Department of Education.

On the day of the test, you will receive a test booklet that contains the essay topics and the numbered test questions, as well as lined paper for the essay and a grid for the multiple-choice questions. You should have plenty of time to complete the examination, but be aware of the amount of time you are spending on each section and each question so that you allow yourself time to complete the test. Although speed is not essential, you should maintain a steady pace. Using the practice tests in this guide will help prepare you to work within the time limits of the examination.

Can I Take the Test Online?

As of this writing, computer-based testing is not available for the FTCE English 6–12. To verify this, go to *www.cefe.usf.edu/* and click on "Computer-Based Testing." Exams on the computer have the advantage of providing you with a notice of pass or fail immediately after completing the exam, which can be scheduled at a time that is convenient for you.

TEST-TAKING TIPS

Although you may not be familiar with tests like the FTCE, this book will acquaint you with this type of exam and help alleviate your test-taking anxieties. By following the seven suggestions listed here, you can become more relaxed about taking the FTCE, as well as other tests.

Tip 1. Become comfortable with the format of the FTCE. When you are practicing, stay calm and pace yourself. After simulating the test only once, you will boost your chances of doing well, and you will be able to sit down for the actual FTCE with much more confidence.

Tip 2. Read all the possible answers. Just because you think you have found the correct response, do not automatically assume that it is the best answer. Read through each choice to be sure that you are not making a mistake by jumping to conclusions.

Tip 3. Use the process of elimination. Go through each answer to a question and eliminate as many of the answer choices as possible. If you can eliminate two answer choices, you have given yourself a better chance of getting the item correct, because only two choices are left from which to make your guess. Do not leave an answer blank; it is better to guess than not to answer a question on the FTCE test.

Tip 4. Place a question mark in your answer booklet next to the answers you guessed, and then recheck them later if you have time.

Tip 5. Work quickly and steadily. You will have two and one-half hours to complete the test, so avoid focusing too long on any one problem. Taking the practice tests in this book will help you learn to budget your precious time.

Tip 6. Learn the directions and format of the test. This will not only save time but also help you avoid anxiety (and the mistakes caused by getting anxious).

Tip 7. When taking the multiple-choice portion of the test, be sure that the answer oval you fill in corresponds to the number of the question in the test booklet. The multiple-choice test is graded by machine, and marking one wrong answer can throw off your answer key and your score. Be extremely careful.

THE DAY OF THE TEST

Before the Test

On the morning of the test, be sure to dress comfortably so you are not distracted by being too hot or too cold while taking the test. Plan to arrive at the test center early. This will allow you to collect your thoughts and relax before the test and will also spare you the anguish that comes with being late. You should check your FTCE Registration Bulletin to find out what time to arrive at the center.

Before you leave for the test center, make sure that you have your admission ticket and two forms of identification, one of which must contain a recent photograph, your name, and your signature (e.g., your driver's license). You will not be admitted to the test center if you do not have proper identification. You must bring several sharpened No. 2 pencils with erasers, because none will be provided at the test center.

If you like, you can wear a watch to the test center. However, you cannot wear one that makes noise, because it might disturb the other test takers. Dictionaries, textbooks, notebooks, calculators, briefcases, or packages will not be permitted. Drinking, smoking, and eating during the test are prohibited.

During the Test

The FTCE English 6–12 is given in one sitting, with no breaks. Procedures will be followed to maintain test security. Once you enter the test center, follow all the rules and instructions given by the test supervisor. If you do not, you risk being dismissed from the test and having your score canceled.

When all the materials have been distributed, the test instructor will give you directions for completing the informational portion of your answer sheet. Fill out the sheet carefully, because the information you provide will be printed on your score report.

Once the test begins, mark only one answer per question, completely erase unwanted answers and marks, and fill in answers darkly and neatly.

After the Test

When you finish your test, hand in your materials and you will be dismissed. Then, go home and relax—you deserve it!

Knowledge of the English Language and Methods for Effective Teaching

2

INFLUENCES ON THE ENGLISH LANGUAGE

Over the course of its long history, the English language has undergone numerous changes. Some alterations were the result of historical, social, cultural, ethnic, religious, regional, or gender influences. A prospective teacher seeking the most all-inclusive knowledge on which to base instruction needs to possess a comprehensive understanding of those influences over time.

Influence of History

Over the last 1,500 years, many cultural groups have been in contact with one another, and their respective political, economic, and social forces have affected the current form of the English language. The aspects of language that have undergone change include differences in the meanings of words, the pronunciation and accenting of spoken language, and the conventions of grammar. Here is one description of some of the early influences on the English language:

> The Roman Christianizing of Britain in 597 brought England into contact with Latin civilization and made significant additions to our vocabulary. The Scandinavian invasions resulted in a considerable mixture of the two peoples and their languages. The Norman Conquest made English for two

centuries the language mainly of the lower classes while the nobles and those associated with them used French on almost all occasions. And when English once more regained supremacy as the language of all elements of the population, it was an English greatly changed in both form and vocabulary from what it had been in 1066. (Baugh and Cable 2002, 2)

Additional historical influences include the Hundred Years' War; the rise of the middle class; the Renaissance; England's emergence as a naval power; the global growth of the British Empire; and the growth of commerce, industry, science, and literature.

Influence of Growth and Change

The fact that the English language continues to change through both growth and decay indicates that it is indeed a living language as opposed to a so-called dead language like Latin, which has remained unchanged for some 2,000 years. The most apparent changes in a living language take place in vocabulary. Old words die out or change in meaning while new words are added. For example, the word *consumption* was most frequently used to refer to the disease tuberculosis. Now that word most often refers to the act of eating or using something up. Scientific discoveries are also responsible for changes or additions to the vocabulary of a language. One recent example is the abbreviation DNA, which stands for *deoxyribonucleic acid*, a constituent of the chromosome that carries genes as segments and can be used to identify individuals who may be crime suspects by a method termed genetic fingerprinting (*Webster's College Dictionary* 1999).

In addition to science, medicine is responsible for contributing new terms like *mad cow disease* and *artificial life*. Computer technology has added many new words, such as *browser*, *Java*, *search engine*, and *Web site*. Fields generally grouped under the arts and entertainment have provided us with words like *audiobook*, *body double*, *DVD*, and *karaoke*.

Other sources of changes in the English language include modifications in social attitudes. For instance, approaches toward women, minorities, and the disadvantaged have brought about terms like *sexism*, *women's liberation*, *black power*, *tokenism*, and *reverse discrimination*. In addition, the recently recognized gay and lesbian subculture has added meaning to the word *gay*, which is often used to replace the term *queer* or *homosexual*.

The fields of physical fitness and bodybuilding have produced their own terminology, including *aerobics*, *Jazzercise*, and *Pilates*. Sports have generated terms like *extreme sports*, *bungee jumping*, and *fantasy football*.

Additional sources of new vocabulary include astronomical research (*black hole*), military engagements (*Patriot missile*), space exploration (*lunar module*), fashion (*supermodel*), and transportation (*HOV lane*).

Influence of Other Languages

Another contributor of vocabulary to the English language is the extensive list of words that have been "borrowed" from foreign languages. Some of these words were added so long ago that their foreign origins have been forgotten. For example, in an English dictionary containing approximately 80,000 entries, almost 30 percent of the words would be recognized as having French origins. Terms like *cordon bleu* and *au gratin*, as well as *garage* and *chauffeur*, have been incorporated from French.

Spanish is responsible for providing us with *paella*, *siesta*, *plaza*, *salsa*, and many other terms in common use. Italian has lent us musical vocabulary such as *fortissimo* and *piano*. Italian culture has provided us with *pizza*, *gondola*, and *balcony*. German has added words relating to the two World Wars, such as *blitz*, and some that people tend to think of as very American, such as *hamburger* and *frankfurter*. Other German-based words in everyday use among English-speaking people include *kindergarten* and *rucksack*. Scandinavian languages have contributed *sky* and *troll*, while Dutch has added sailing terms like *skipper* and *keel*. Russian is responsible for adding, for example, *Cossack* and *babushka* to the English vocabulary.

Latin words are primarily related to biological, medical, and legal terminology. Greek has given English medical terminology, particularly the various phobias and "ologies" that make up school curricula. Arabic has given English religious terms such as *jihad* as well as some scientific vocabulary originally borrowed from Latin during the Middle Ages, such as *alcohol* and *algebra*. India has supplied *pajamas*, *jungle*, *shampoo*, and *khaki*.

Because the English language has seemingly endless sources of new words, its continued modification and expansion is assured.

VARIOUS APPROACHES TO THE STUDY OF LANGUAGE AND KNOWLEDGE OF STANDARD WRITTEN ENGLISH

Students can learn about language by studying grammar, writing and speaking styles, and usage. The importance of grammar is clear from the following definition:

> *Grammar* is most simply defined as "a description of how English works." Through a process of analysis, the grammarian discovers the various components or parts of the language system and how they fit together. Grammar is a description of the language conventions that a speaker of the language has mastered in order to communicate with other people. Grammar is not a set of rules telling how one is "supposed" to speak, and it does not prescribe behavior. It simply makes note of the language behavior that native speakers have learned. Very few people actually speak "ungrammatically," because something that is ungrammatical does not follow the basic patterns of English and therefore cannot be understood by another person. (Tchudi and Mitchell 1999, 297)

Traditional Grammar

In the United States, grammar is the most widely taught area of study in the language arts. Nevertheless, it is the least understood component and the most controversial in terms of best practices or effective instructional techniques. When American adults think back to the English classes they took in school, they recall learning grammar by memorizing terminology and rules, diagramming sentences, completing worksheets by filling in the blanks, and taking numerous quizzes. These activities were the focus of grammar instruction because they were thought to equip students to speak and write acceptable or "correct" English. However, a wealth of research indicates that engaging in these activities does little to effect student competency and performance (Maxwell and Meiser 1997).

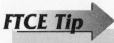

FTCE Tip

Skills practiced in isolation don't transfer to essay writing.

Having students practice these skills in isolation, completing textbook activities or worksheets, simply does not achieve the desired aim because the skills fail to transfer when students are required to write on their own. Learning of this sort is not stored in long-term memory, so even the student who achieves a perfect score on a test covering recently learned language skills is likely to make errors in the same skills when writing an essay the following week. Further, the context in which people use language dictates the choices they make about correct or appropriate language. The ability to correctly complete a worksheet or to correct errors in sentences provided on a test has little bearing on the context in which students actually use language, because those activities are devoid of context. In addition, noncontextual material is usually much simpler than the language students normally use, and the time spent working on such material limits the time students can engage in actual writing. Thus, they are not occupied in the kind of communication in which the skills they learned are meaningful and can help them express the ideas most important to them (Maxwell and Meiser 1997).

If research shows that traditional methods of teaching grammar fail, why do teachers continue to engage in them? One reason is that people continue to believe that studying grammar facilitates the ability to use language correctly. Further, many people consider the study of grammar as genuine schooling because they recall their own experiences when such study was the standard for literacy. They fail to recognize that true literacy comes about because of a compendium of active listening, speaking, reading, and writing. Students also need to be motivated to become literate and to be placed in an environment that supports literacy.

Another reason for the persistence of traditional grammar instruction is many language arts or English teachers believe that their own superior skills in this area resulted from their participating in such instruction. These teachers fail to recognize that they demonstrated a particular affinity for language, were most likely highly motivated, and probably received considerable reinforcement in these areas.

A third reason is that textbooks and other pedagogical materials are readily available to support traditional grammar instruction. By nature, most English teachers enjoy teaching grammar and select instructional materials that reinforce what they are most comfortable doing. As long as this continues, traditional grammar instruction will continue, despite its many shortcomings.

Structural Grammar

Many English teachers have abandoned traditional grammar in favor of structural grammar, which may be seen as more closely linked to reading instruction. Traditional grammar instructors teach rules dictating what should or should not be done to construct sentences. Structural grammar views language as comprising three distinct levels: individual sounds, groups of sounds, and groups of words. The study of the sounds of language is called *phonology*; the study of groups of sounds that, when put together, provide meaning is termed *morphology*; and the arrangement of words, bearing in mind their relationship to one another, is the *syntax* of language.

Structural grammar facilitates both teaching and learning. In traditional grammar, a noun is typically defined as "the name of a person, place, or thing," which fails to adequately account for terms like *justice* and *liberty*, which are complex concepts that are difficult to explain to adults much less children. Traditionalists define verbs as words that connote "actions or states of being." It would be very difficult at best to explain a "state of being" to a young student. The problem is eliminated in structural grammar by identifying a verb by its inflectional ending, which indicates tense. A verb is also identified by its place in a sentence, typically at the beginning of the predicate. Further, structuralists categorize adverbs and adjectives by their characteristic endings and by the uses made of them.

FTCE Tip

A "state of being" is very hard to explain!

Language arts teachers who employ structural grammar find it far simpler to have their students relate to the specific functions of words in sentences than to definitions of terms that are often difficult to comprehend, particularly in complex sentences (Maxwell and Meiser 1997).

Transformational Grammar

A third approach to grammar instruction is transformational grammar. This method uses basic or kernel sentences that are transformed or changed into various patterns. The result of this pedagogical system is the construction of either kernel or transformed sentences. A kernel sentence might be "The wagon is red." Transformations of that basic sentence could include a negative ("The wagon is not red"), a question ("Is the wagon red?"), a passive ("The wagon was painted red"), or an embedded phrase ("The wagon that belonged to Carol was red").

Language arts teachers have found transformational grammar useful for teaching their students how to rewrite sentences and combine them. This instructional approach has made students more aware of syntax, the effectiveness of language, and the function of various forms of punctuation.

Any approach to grammar instruction in isolation is bound to fail in certain areas. Although structural grammar seems superior to traditional instruction and transformational grammar seems to be an improvement on the structural approach, students need to spend the most time on creating their own written text, where the connection between grammar and conveying intended meaning to the reader is clear. Otherwise, students tend to see grammar as another content area to be mastered for success on tests, one that is disliked intensely and unconnected to their own ability to write.

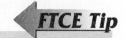

FTCE Tip

Teaching grammar in isolation is not enough.

Another aspect of the English language that needs to be demystified for students is the concept of and appropriate application of usage. *Usage* has been defined as "a range of socially significant choices available to a speaker within the grammar of a language. . . . [Usage] is a sociological phenomenon, not primarily linguistic, which means that it is concerned with the perceived social level of the speaker rather than with understanding or communication of messages" (Tchudi and Mitchell 1999, 298). Many people confuse grammar and usage, and those who depart from standard dialect are often accused of having bad grammar. The presumption that studying grammar will eliminate usage problems and "correct" how people write and speak is incorrect and only results in wasted efforts and frustrated students.

Some researchers of language arts instruction claim that there is no such thing as correct usage, because the purpose of written and oral language is to communicate meaning; as long as meaning is conveyed, usage is irrelevant. Moreover, usage pertains to the range of dialects that exist in English. Dialects should be viewed as varieties or styles of language that refer to differences in pronunciation, usage, and vocabulary. Some of the better-known dialects of English include Ebonics, Yankee, Southern, Appalachian, Valley Girl, Brooklynese, and others (Tchundi and Mitchell 1999). Every dialect works well because each serves the communication needs of its users. However, each dialect is unique in terms of the prestige it affords its users. This is the primary reason that schools attempt to teach standard usage, which is how those from the middle and upper classes use language. However, the concept of standard usage remains, and most teachers feel that departures from this standard must be corrected. The mastery of this standard form is thought to enable students to advance to higher social levels and to achieve employment that would be denied them if they spoke only a nonstandard dialect.

Because of the social realities of various dialects, teachers sometimes tread in dangerous waters, reluctant to correct a student's "mistakes" because they do not want to be critical or to deprecate some dialects while praising others. Further, some students have learned to use appropriate dialects depending on the setting in which they find themselves. For example, some retain a home or family dialect for use outside a school or business setting and employ standard dialect when it suits their purpose. This enables them to succeed in school or business without offending family and friends who may use a nonstandard dialect.

FTCE Tip

Students can learn when to use a dialect.

In terms of written English, Standard English and its conventions are taught. Students whose backgrounds are not American often have trouble putting their thoughts on paper. People tend to write as they speak, so teachers find that students who speak nonstandard English or who learned English as a second language have more difficulty with written English than other students, because speaking and writing are closely intertwined.

Further, students who are learning English as a second language have a difficult time grappling with usage and often fail to grasp its meaning or importance. One way to define usage is by example. Because it is too complex to define abstractly or out of context, usage can be effectively defined by example. Consider, for instance, a class for English language learners who were assigned to read an interesting newspaper article and then rewrite it in their own words. One student completed the task using a story about a fire in a high-rise apartment building. He wrote about the heroic fireman who climbed a ladder into the burning building and emerged pregnant! The student submitting this summary was obviously unaware that the word *pregnant* has a very specific meaning in English and can never be applied to men. In addition, although a dictionary would define the term as "with child" or "carrying a child," the external carrying of a child does not fit the definition. Therefore, the student made a classic error in usage, one that might be difficult to explain, and one that it is unlikely to be avoided by someone just learning the language.

HOW AUDIENCE AND PURPOSE AFFECT LANGUAGE

When learning the language arts, students should become aware that their intended purpose and the audience they are targeting significantly affect the language they use in their speaking and writing.

Teachers often use far more specific language in the classroom than they do in other situations. To help ensure that students understand the lesson, the teacher is conscious of communicating ideas as clearly as possible and defining terms either by incorporating definitions or by providing useful context clues. When presenting a lesson orally, the teacher might be intentionally repetitive to reinforce concepts. The same teacher, engaged in a conversation on the same topic with someone who already knows something about it, would use language in a very different way.

In addition, the language a person would use to impart new knowledge is very different from the language that person would use to persuade an audience, which in turn is quite unlike the language used to entertain listeners or readers. Students need to consider their audience and to have specific practice in addressing these different groups.

METHODS OF EFFECTIVELY ASSESSING LANGUAGE SKILLS

The terms *assessment*, *evaluation*, and *grading*, though often used interchangeably, have distinct meanings. *Assessment*, the broadest of the three terms, refers to the tools a teacher uses to obtain an overall view of how a student is progressing. Thus, assessment allows the teacher to see that a student has shown improvement in the various communication skills from one assignment to the next, that no such improvement is evident, or that the student has regressed in skill development. Evaluation, on the other hand, requires judging the quality of a piece of work. Therefore, when evaluating how a student performed on a specific task, a teacher determines that the performance was poor, fair, good, or excellent. Finally, grading is a specific task that every teacher is required to perform. Using the results of the assessment and evaluation, a teacher assigns a letter or numerical grade to the student's work.

The whole area of assessment (the term used in this book because it is the broadest and generally incorporates the other two) is highly controversial. There are many approaches to assessment, some superior to others and some more appropriate to certain tasks than to others. In addition, it is important to consider the purpose of assessment before selecting the most suitable method.

Teachers should directly link assessment to curriculum, but often the reverse happens. Because of the emphasis on state standards and standardized testing, teachers find themselves teaching test content rather than the appropriate English language arts curriculum.

In Florida, the ratings of students, teachers, and schools are based on student performance on a series of tests. It is understandable and, to a certain degree, necessary that students are well prepared to perform well on these tests; promotion and high school graduation depend on it.

Tools for Assessment

Rubric

One effective tool to assess language skills is the rubric. In general, a rubric is a scoring guide that focuses on specific aspects of an assignment or task. It divides the task into various components, enabling the teacher to analyze and evaluate the presence or absence of each. Sometimes task components are weighted, meaning that some are afforded more importance than others, often in recognition of the effort or time required for each.

Checklist

A simple and often-used assessment tool is the checklist. A checklist is used to record whether or not a task has been performed. For example, a checklist used to evaluate a book report might indicate whether the student included the author's name, the copyright date, the complete title of the book, and the name and location of the publisher. Anything else that can be reduced to a yes/no or present/absent format is appropriate for inclusion on a checklist. While not nearly as informative as a rubric or some other assessment tools, checklists serve their own limited purposes well and are frequently used.

Anecdotal Record

Another useful form of assessment is the anecdotal record. This type of assessment requires the teacher to observe the student and record, as soon as possible after the observation, an account of exactly what took place. For example, a teacher observing a particular student during a classroom discussion might note afterward, "Lisa, for the first time, contributed to the discussion as an active participant." Although obviously useful as a record of actual performance or activity, anecdotal records can be unintentionally biased. To minimize or eliminate bias, an anecdotal record should separate the facts of the observation from the teacher's interpretations of the event. It is also important that the teacher keep anecdotal records on all students, not just those who stand out for either

FTCE Tip
Some recordings of students could be biased.

negative or positive reasons. In this way, the teacher will have information on all students and will be able to use this to tailor lessons and individualize assignments.

Running Record

Another observational tool that can contribute to the assessment of a student's language skills is the running record. One form of running record is the informal reading inventory (IRI). This type of informal assessment was once teacher-made but is now commercially available. The IRI is defined as

> a series of graded passages, increasing in difficulty, used to determine a child's reading level for both word identification and comprehension. It enables you to observe strengths and weaknesses, as well as gain insights about individual readers. The primary purpose for using IRIs is to diagnose difficulties and provide appropriate instruction directed toward the skills children lack. (Roe and Ross 2006, 518–519)

The IRI reveals to the teacher four levels of reading or reading-related performance: (1) the independent reading level, at which the student recognizes at least 99 percent of the words presented and has at least a 90 percent level of comprehension; (2) the instructional level, at which the student recognizes 95 percent of the words presented and has a comprehension level of 75 percent; and (3) the frustration level, at which the student recognizes less than 90 percent of the words provided and demonstrates a comprehension level of less than 50 percent. Finally, the fourth level of performance that an IRI yields, called *capacity*, indicates the student's listening comprehension level. This level is reached when the student understands 75 percent of what he or she heard. Students should be working with material at their instructional level when the teacher is working with them and is available to offer support and assistance. When students select books to read during leisure time or when the teacher is not available to help, they should be reading books at the independent level.

Writing Samples

The assessment of written English is best based on writing samples collected under various circumstances. For example, sometimes students should be given the opportunity for free writing, or writing on a topic of their choice. On occasion, the student should also be allowed to choose the format of a free-writing assignment. For example, the student might choose to write a poem for one assignment and an essay for another. At other times, the student should be required to write in response to a prompt, and part of the assessment of that writing would be related to how well the written work addresses the issue or issues raised by the prompt. For example, given a prompt concerned with the benefits of cooperation as opposed to competition, the student who dealt only with competition would not be assessed as highly as the student who addressed both concepts and compared and contrasted them well.

The type of assessment performed on student writing can also take various forms depending on the teacher's purpose. For example, one assessment might help the teacher evaluate students' ability to spell correctly, while another assessment would target the use of correct capitalization or punctuation. Using a checklist or rubric, mentioned earlier, a teacher can easily record specific errors that can then become the focal point of additional group (if many students are making the same types of errors) or individual remedial instruction. The teacher can also use a checklist or rubric during a specific activity such as an oral presentation or class discussion to evaluate students' listening skills, such as their ability to follow oral instructions, make pertinent remarks, or ask relevant questions during or following the presentation or discussion.

Assessing Vocabulary and Spelling

Vocabulary and spelling should not be assessed in isolation because doing so takes the words out of context and focuses on only the words. Most students can "learn" how to spell selected words and retain that knowledge long enough to do well on a spelling test. The same is true of "learning" the definitions of specific vocabulary words. However, this level of knowledge, aside from perhaps leading to a good grade on a test, is not useful and is not retained or applied across subjects. Rather, when presenting students with new vocabulary, the teacher should give them the opportunity to hear, see, and use each new word correctly at least 10 times so they incorporate the word into their own vocabulary. Vocabulary should be evaluated in the context of all the language arts.

- Can the student use appropriate vocabulary while engaged in conversation or when writing a response to a prompt?

- Does the student make appropriate responses to questions about words encountered in a reading selection?

- How appropriate is the student's response to specific spoken words?

The teacher's evaluation should focus on the student's ability to interpret and to apply selected vocabulary.

Speaking skills can be evaluated in two distinct ways: informally through observation and formally by means of a structured evaluation tool. Rating scales have been developed for this language skill, such as the Teacher Rating of Oral Language and Literacy (TROLL; Roe and Ross 2006). This tool helps the teacher evaluate the student's ability to start a conversation, ask questions, use varied vocabulary, and so on. Informally, the teacher can carefully observe a student's oral expression, focusing on skills included on a checklist or rubric, and then either indicate whether the student demonstrates those skills (checklist) or evaluate the quality of each skill (rubric).

Taping Students

Another way to assess speaking skills is to audiotape or videotape students on a periodic basis. Tapes allow the teacher to listen to students as many times as needed to pinpoint specific strengths and weaknesses. However, unless they are taped rather frequently, students can become self-conscious and either refuse to participate or do so in a very atypical manner. Because the purpose of this tool is evaluating realistic oral language, self-conscious contributions will not be helpful.

Portfolios

Portfolios are also an effective way to evaluate the development of language skills. As a type of authentic assessment, a portfolio is an organized (usually chronological) collection of students' work over a specific period. Because a portfolio contains a collection of work, it enables the teacher, the student, and parents to see patterns of development and progress. Generally, when a student begins a portfolio, the selection of work to be included is a cooperative exercise between the student and the teacher. After gaining some experience with portfolios, the class can develop specific selection criteria, and each student can apply those criteria independently. It is important that the items selected not include only examples of the student's best work. Instead, various pieces, including both the draft and final versions of the same writing assignment, should be included to show the student's development through revisions and editing. Requiring the student to attach to each item his or her rationale for including that particular piece will lead the student to reflect on how the work demonstrates growth. Although student writing is probably the type of work most often kept in a portfolio, any piece that demonstrates student effort is appropriate for a portfolio. Portfolios can take many physical forms, including folders, three-ring binders, expandable folders, or boxes.

FTCE Tip

Don't put just the "best" work in a portfolio.

METHODS AND STRATEGIES FOR TEACHING ENGLISH FOR SPEAKERS OF OTHER LANGUAGES

Teachers who work with children for whom English is a second language need to keep in mind that second-language learners often give the appearance of possessing greater mastery of English than they actually possess. This happens because most of these students learn what is now commonly called BICS (Basic Interpersonal Communicative Skills). BICS has been defined as "the basic communicative fluency achieved by all normal native speakers of a language. It is cognitively undemanding and contextual and is better understood as the language used by students in informal settings, say on the playground" (Cummins 2003, 322). Research suggests that it typically takes language learners just one to three years to develop BICS if they have sufficient exposure to the second language.

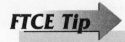

FTCE Tip

Students need to be able to think in a language to use it as a tool for learning.

Another tool that many English-language learners use is called CALP (Cognitive Academic Language Proficiency). Students use CALP while performing in an academic setting. It is the ability to think in and use a language as a tool for learning. Because CALP involves using abstractions in a sophisticated manner to manipulate language, students in grades K–12 who have native language literacy need five to seven years to acquire it. Learners who do not have strong native language literacy often need seven to ten years to acquire CALP in the second language.

Students need to master CALP to be able to use English as a tool for learning rather than just for conversational purposes. Many experts in the field of second-language acquisition are now advocating the integration of language and content as a way of decreasing the amount of time students need to develop CALP. In addition, teachers should use the following specific strategies when working with second-language learners: teacher talk, body language, explicit language modeling, the presentation of realia, and the incorporation of visuals and manipulatives. Further, teachers should use predictable instructional routines and build redundancy into lessons.

It is generally accepted procedure for students to interact to produce comprehensible output. Teachers need to encourage student interaction. Strategies to do so include using appropriate questioning strategies, drawing on students' background knowledge, using clarification and comprehension checks, paraphrasing, and enriching and elaborating students' utterances (or asking students to do so). In addition, teachers are encouraged to use group work, class presentations, discussions, and debates. New vocabulary should be taught in every subject. According to one researcher, "Vocabulary knowledge in English is the most important aspect of oral English proficiency for academic achievement" (Saville-Troike 1984, 216). Providing a list of new vocabulary at the start of a unit of instruction is not sufficient because at that point the words serve no purpose for the students and are not yet associated with meanings. Hands-on experiences or experiences with concrete objects, pictures, and other visuals, followed by pertinent discussion, are necessary for effective vocabulary instruction. To check students' comprehension of new terms, the teacher should ask students to reuse each new word in different contexts (Seal 1991).

References

Baugh, A. C., and T. Cable. 2002. *A history of the English language.* 5th ed. London: Routledge.

Cummins, J. 2003. *BICS and CALP: Origins and rationale for the distinction.* In *Sociolinguistics: The essential readings*, ed. C. B. Paulston and G. G. Tucker, 322–328. London: Blackwell.

Maxwell, R. J., and M. J. Meiser. 1997. *Teaching English in middle and secondary schools.* 2nd ed. Upper Saddle River, NJ: Prentice Hall.

Roe, B. C., and E. P. Ross. 2006. *Integrating language arts through literature and thematic units.* Boston: Allyn & Bacon.

Saville-Troike, M. 1984. What really matters in second language learning for academic achievement? *TESOL Quarterly* 17: 199–219.

Seal, B. D. 1991. *Vocabulary learning and teaching.* In *Teaching English as a second or foreign language*, ed. M. Celce-Murcia, 296–311. Boston: Newbury House.

Tchudi, S., and D. Mitchell. 1999. *Exploring and teaching the English language arts.* 4th ed. New York: Longman.

Webster's college dictionary. 1999. New York: Random House.

CHAPTER 3

Knowledge of Writing and Methods for Effective Teaching

TECHNIQUES TO DEVELOP A SUPPORTIVE CLASSROOM ENVIRONMENT FOR WRITING

Anyone attempting to teach students to write well must recognize that oral language always precedes written language. Therefore, to be effective in developing proficient writers, teachers must first develop proficient speakers, allocating classroom time to the development and refinement of oral language before attempting to develop and refine written language. A silent classroom may impress an uninitiated administrator but will do little or nothing to encourage students' language skills.

Writing does not come naturally to most people; it requires instruction and many opportunities to practice and to receive constructive feedback. Unfortunately, many classrooms are overcrowded, and many teachers are forced to work with more than one large class. As a result, students are afforded fewer opportunities to write, and teachers are handicapped in their ability to provide detailed, informative, and useful feedback to their students. Despite these often adverse conditions, however, teachers must provide a supportive environment if they truly want to encourage their students to write and to improve their writing skills. "Students need a classroom framework that supports their development as writers. A framework allows them to function as a community of writers and should consist of rules and expectations, routines, schedules, writing folders, portfolios, and schedules" (Oglan 2003, 93).

Techniques

Peer Sharing

Students should be encouraged to discuss and to share their writing with their class-mates as well as their teacher. But first both the teacher and the student need to develop a set of rules to govern the freedom this sharing process demands. The student must be involved in establishing these rules. "When you involve students in the setting of writing expectations, they take ownership of the writing environment" (Oglan 2003, 94). Here is a suggested set of rules:

1. Be patient and wait my turn.
2. Try to solve my own problems before involving others.
3. Give help to others when asked.
4. Try to edit and revise my own work to the best of my ability.
5. Confer with others about suggested edits and revisions after I have finished editing and revising my own work.
6. Speak in a low, respectful voice so as not to interfere with the work of others.
7. Try not to do anything that might distract or disturb others.
8. Recognize that mistakes will be made, and learn to accept and to learn from them.
9. Act cooperatively rather than competitively.

These are recommended as applicable to most classrooms, but a classroom might require additional rules to meet specific needs, and new rules can be added when such special situations arise.

Use of Routines

Students need and appreciate routines because they provide a sense of security. To develop writers, teachers need to establish both procedural and organizational routines at the very start of the school year. Procedurally, it is important that students be made aware of the writing schedule. Writing will not necessarily be part of each class session but should not be sprung on students; they should be able to anticipate it and to gear up for it psychologically. Organizational routines would include establishing a storage area for writing supplies, folders, and portfolios. Although students should be expected to supply their own writing materials, no student lacking the needed supplies should be excluded from a writing experience. Further, students who are reluctant writers might intentionally "forget" their materials to avoid participating. The strategy of having supplies available in class should preclude this avoidance technique.

FTCE Tip

Having writing supplies in the classroom will promote more writing.

Schedules need to be developed that allow enough time to accommodate all facets of the writing process and what is called the *authoring cycle*. This would include time for students to construct their rough drafts, share their work with peers, revise, edit, and possibly publish their work. A language arts teacher in a self-contained classroom, responsible for teaching all or many of the core subjects, can find time for the authoring cycle by integrating writing experiences with other subjects such as science and social studies. On the other hand, anyone teaching language arts or English as a separate subject needs to devote as much time as possible to writing, as frequently as possible, perhaps integrating it with literature. A teacher can also ask colleagues who teach other subjects to incorporate writing in their classrooms to clarify and solidify concepts. In that way, the English or language arts teacher is not solely responsible for students' writing progress, and students benefit from opportunities to engage in writing across the curriculum.

Writing Folders

One way to help students organize their writing efforts is to furnish them with writing folders. In addition to the completed writing pieces, the students' folder can store works in progress, CDs used to electronically store computer-generated writing, illustrations and other artwork to accompany the writing, notes, lists of resources, and anything students might find useful for future projects. It is important for the teacher and students to work together in establishing and adhering to a system of storing, distributing, and organizing these folders so they can always be readily retrieved when needed.

As mentioned earlier, teachers often use writing portfolios in the assessment of student writing. These are a part of the writing environment and are used to track the progression of students' development as writers. Keep in mind that each piece of work selected for the portfolio—by the student, by you, or jointly—should be date-stamped and filed in chronological order.

Supportive Environment

In general, a supportive environment for writing is safe and encourages writers to take risks and try their best without fear of negative repercussions. Teachers are responsible for creating this type of atmosphere.

TECHNIQUES FOR TEACHING STUDENTS TO MAKE EFFECTIVE ORGANIZATIONAL AND STYLISTIC CHOICES

A common problem among students learning to write is the tendency to compose rambling, repetitive pieces that are generally or thoroughly not well organized. Another problem is the lack of style or a monotonous style. *Style* can be defined as "the characteristic way of writing that distinguishes one writer from another" (*Macmillan English* 1998, 127). The role of the language arts teacher includes teaching students to make effective organizational and stylistic choices.

Organization

Language arts teachers should guide students in organizing their writing in chronological, spatial, or developmental order; in order of importance; or by comparing and contrasting.

Narratives

Students can learn to use chronological order by practicing writing narratives, which are real or imaginary stories that have a clear beginning, middle, and end. When organizing their writing in chronological order, students should use appropriate transitions, such as *after*, *later*, *immediately*, *before*, *when*, *as soon as*, *during*, *until*, *at last*, *finally*, and *next* (Senn and Skinner 1995, 105). The teacher can give students additional practice by giving them a list of specific events, written in random order, to reorganize into chronological order. For example, the teacher could list the following events and ask students to organize them correctly (Senn and Skinner 1995, 105):

- I came into the house to measure the rainwater I had collected.
- I kept a weather station for a science project two years ago.
- I went to check the cup to see how much rain we had had.

- The doctor numbed my finger and then gave me stitches.

- I wrapped a cold washcloth around my bleeding finger.

- I slipped on the wet floor, and the cup broke in my hand.

- We had a heavy rainfall.

- My mother rushed me to the emergency clinic.

- The stitches were removed one week later.

- We had to spend an hour in the waiting room.

Descriptions

Practice in writing descriptive paragraphs will help students learn spatial organization. A descriptive paragraph is one that "paints a vivid picture of a person, an object, or a scene by using sensory details" (Senn and Skinner 1995, 109). The topic sentence of this type of paragraph communicates to the reader a strong impression of a person, a scene, or an object. Sensory details are used in supportive sentences to show, rather than tell, the reader details pertaining to the subject matter.

In addition to rich sensory details, descriptive paragraphs use figurative language to form a picture for the reader. This type of writing enables students to make use of and learn more about similes and metaphors. A simile is a comparison of two very different things using *as* or *like*. An example of a simile is "as white as snow." A metaphor indicates a comparison but does so directly, without the use of *as* or *like*. An example of a metaphor is "rock hard." The use of figurative language makes writing richer and more colorful.

In a descriptive paragraph, the writer is leading the reader on a journey. For the reader to follow along, the writer must arrange details in spatial order, or according to their location in relation to each other. Spatial order can be from top to bottom (or the reverse) and uses transitions like *higher*, *lower*, *above*, *below*, *underneath*, *on top of*, and so on. Spatial order might also be from side to side and would use transitions such as *at the right* (or *left*), *in the middle*, *next to*, and so forth. Inside out or outside in is another spatial order a writer might employ. In that case, transitions such a *within*, *in the center*, *on the outside*, and the like may be used. Finally, near to far or far to near might be the form of spatial organization a writer uses. In that case, transitions like *north*, *south*, *east*, *west*, *nearby*, *in the distance*, *behind*, *at the edge*, *on the horizon*, and so on are appropriate (Senn and Skinner 1995).

Writing Style

In working with students to develop their writing style, a teacher should be looking for precise language—specific words punctuated with vivid modifiers and descriptive phrases. Another indicator of a writer's style is the use of appropriate connotations that do a good job of getting across intended meaning. Further, evidence of a writer's style comes from correct and appropriate use of similes, metaphors, personification, and onomatopoeia. *Personification* is a comparison that gives an object or idea human or animal qualities. One example of personification is in *Alice's Adventures in Wonderland.* When Alice is trying to follow the white rabbit, she has to go through a small door, one that she is clearly too large to enter. She tries the doorknob, which then says, "Ouch! You gave me quite a turn!" Obviously, a doorknob cannot feel pain or speak, but with personification, it does both. Finally, *onomatopoeia* is the use of words whose sounds suggest their meanings. Words such as *splash*, *hum*, *moo*, *click*, *fizz*, and *plop* are all examples of onomatopoeia. Writers who use a variety of these devices develop an interesting style that keeps a reader focused and motivated to continue reading.

Clichés

Another way writers can establish their style is to avoid clichés, which are trite, overused phrases that detract from good writing. Examples of clichés are *hungry as a wolf*, *crystal clear*, *pretty as a picture*, *sweet as honey*, *cool as ice*, *smooth as silk* (Senn and Skinner 1995, 61). Teachers need to instruct students to substitute new figurative language for these overused expressions.

Wordiness

Many students benefit from instruction in writing concise sentences, because they tend to write in a rambling, wordy manner. Some of the elements of wordiness are redundancy, empty expressions, inflated language, and the use of jargon.

Redundancy is unnecessary repetition. Stating that, "You should avoid taking dangerous risks" is redundant because by definition all risks are dangerous. *Wordiness* is the use of more words than are necessary to communicate an idea. Such uneconomical writing detracts rather than enhances writing, so teach students to write more to the point. Here is an example of a wordy sentence: "Students who cannot successfully function in a mathematical learning situation must be reprocessed until they acquire this skill." This sentence should be rewritten as "Students who fail mathematics courses must repeat these courses until they pass" (Senn and Skinner 1995, 65).

Empty expressions are "phrases that add no meaning to a sentence." To improve students' writing style, teachers need to show them how to eliminate empty expressions or replace them with single words or concise phrases. Empty expressions include the following: *on account of, due to the fact that, what I want is, the reason is because, in my opinion, what I'm trying to say is that, it seems as if, the thing is that, because of the fact that.* The empty expression "It seems as if advertisers often appeal to emotions" should be replaced with "Advertisers often appeal to emotions" (Senn and Skinner 1995, 63).

Inflated language consists of words that sound impressive because they are multisyllabic but do not communicate as effectively as simple, direct words. Teachers should advise students to avoid this type of language and to be more succinct. The following sentence uses inflated language: "The governor has availed herself of every opportu-

FTCE Tip

Multisyllabic words do not say it as well as simple, direct words.

nity to enlarge her knowledge of recently published economic theories" and can be made clearer and more concise by rewriting it as "The governor has studied recent economic theories" (Senn and Skinner 1995, 64).

Finally, students should learn to avoid *jargon*, which is the specialized vocabulary of a group or profession. Jargon is appropriate only when used by a specialist who is writing for or addressing other members of the same specialty. It is inappropriate in school writing when ordinary vocabulary will do a better job of conveying meaning. A writer who uses jargon usually has to "translate" it into ordinary language to make its meaning understood, which results in wordiness. An example of the use of jargon is "The photo had to be cropped so it would not bleed into the gutter," which can be rewritten as "The photograph had to be trimmed so it would not extend beyond the inside margin" (*Macmillan English* 1998, 62).

ELEMENTS OF THE WRITING PROCESS AND ACTIVITIES THAT SUPPORT THE WRITING PROCESS

Teachers need to instruct students to view writing as a process that has six components: prewriting, drafting, revising, editing, proofreading, and publishing.

Prewriting

Prewriting is the planning phase of the writing process. Everything the writer does before creating the first draft is part of this phase. A great deal of thinking happens during this phase. First, the writer thinks about the topic that will become the focus of the piece and delimits the topic so that it is manageable. Then the writer organizes information on the topic along some dimension and then decides on an organizational format. Next, the writer decides on the audience for the piece. Finally, the writer chooses a point of view for the writing (Roe and Ross 2006).

Topic Selection

It is typical for teachers to assign writing topics or to provide prompts to which students must respond. However, writers allowed to select their own topics will feel they are in control, enabling them to write about topics they know about and that matter to them. This will allow students to focus on the writing process rather than on gathering information for the content, which ultimately makes the task of writing easier for them. On some occasions, teachers need to assign topics, such as when students are learning how to write a report or to prepare them for standardized tests like the SAT, which requires them to write on a specific topic.

Strategies for identifying a subject include listing interests and experiences, keeping a personal journal, using pieces of literature for inspiration, and a technique called freewriting (Senn and Skinner 1995). Teachers can use interest inventories (available online or in language arts texts) to assist students in pinpointing their individual interests. These frequently consist of open-ended statements on various subjects for the students to complete. Here are two examples: "When I have some free time, I like to . . ." and "If I could travel to any place in the world, I would visit . . ." Students can file the results of such an inventory in their respective writing folders for use in future writing exercises.

Some teachers have students keep journals in which to write, on a daily basis, their responses to people and events in their lives or in the world at large. In their journals, students can record ideas they want to explore, questions they have, sketches they have made, and words that intrigue them. All journal entries are possible topics for future writing.

Literature with which students are familiar can also serve as a source of inspiration. Students can write about a particular piece of fiction or a poem that they have read. They might want to focus on the plot of a novel or a particular character, the setting, or the theme.

Some students might choose to write their interpretation of a poem, about the message the poet was trying to convey, or about the poet himself.

Freewriting

Freewriting is another technique students can use to reveal topics for future writing assignments. In this approach, students let their minds roam free and write about ideas as they think of them. Another version of this method is called focused freewriting. Using this technique, each student focuses on an idea, word, or phrase and then writes everything possible about the focus topic that comes to mind within a given time limit. The student must continue to write for the entire time. If ideas on the topic cease to flow, the student should just write down anything to keep the flow of writing going. The products of a focused freewriting exercise should be saved in the student's writing folder for future development.

Delimiting a Topic

Students need to learn how to delimit a topic, particularly one of their own choosing, so they can address it in the time allowed or within the word or page limits given. Without this ability, a student is apt to select a topic so broad that the student would need to write an entire book rather than a single paper. The teacher needs to model topic selection and the process of delimiting that topic. Students can then do exercises in delimiting topics provided to them and eventually transfer their ability to delimiting topics of their own choice (Roe and Ross 2006).

Teachers can tell students about the following strategies for delimiting a subject and model them as well: "limit your subject to one person or one example that represents the subject; limit your subject to a specific time or place; limit your subject to a specific event; limit your subject to a specific condition, purpose, or procedure" (Senn and Skinner 1995, 16). Given a list of topics that are too broad, students would attempt to limit them to those that are more reasonable by using each of the strategies just described. Practice of this kind will furnish students with skills they can apply to their future writing experiences.

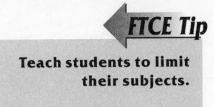

FTCE Tip

Teach students to limit their subjects.

Organizing Thoughts

Strategies that can be taught and then later used to help students to organize their thoughts during the prewriting phase include making lists, semantic webbing, drawing or sketching, and discussion (brainstorming) with their teacher and peers. Teachers need to remind students to engage in one of these activities before starting any writing activity, because most students want to rush into the first draft and skip this organizational step entirely. Requiring students to employ organizational strategies does not ensure that the actual writing will be organized, but it does increase the likelihood.

Purpose

The next element that the writer must consider in the prewriting phase is the purpose of and audience for the finished piece. Some possible purposes for writing include these: to explain or inform; to persuade; to express personal thoughts, feelings, or opinions; or to describe. Sometimes a writer combines two or more of these purposes. For example, writers might provide information to their readers and give a personal opinion about the same subject. In another piece, writers might describe somewhere they have visited and attempt to persuade the reader to travel there as well (Senn and Skinner 1995).

Audience

Writers should also consider the audience that they intend to reach before they start writing. Questions writers should ask themselves concerning their target audience include, "Who will be reading my work? How old are they? Are they adults, teenagers, or children? What background do they have in the subject? What interests and opinions are they likely to have? Are there any words or terms I should define for them?" (Senn and Skinner 1995, 17). Students can be given practice in writing two short pieces on the same subject but directed to two very different audiences. This exercise will make students aware of the types of modifications they would want to make to tailor the piece to the intended readers.

Point of View

The final aspect of a piece of writing that should be considered during the prewriting phase is the point of view. Authors can choose to tell a story, express an opinion, attempt to persuade, or describe something from their own point of view and write the piece in the first person using *I*, *we*, *us*, and *our*. Alternatively, authors might choose to write in the third person using pronouns such as *she*, *he*, *they*, *their*, *his*, or *her*. To give students repeated opportunities to practice writing from both viewpoints, teachers can provide exercises in changing sentences from first to third person or from third to first person. They should also engage in dialogue on the appropriateness of one over the other depending on the purpose of the piece and the intended effect of the completed writing. Writing in the first person often has more of an emotional impact on the reader than does writing in the third person.

Drafting

The next phase in the writing process is drafting. In this phase, writers begin to put their ideas on paper. They use everything they have done in the prewriting phase but should not be terribly concerned, at this point, with word choice or other details and technical aspects of the piece. They will address those concerns later. Some strategies that teachers can suggest students use to draft their pieces include the following:

> Write an introduction that will capture the reader's interest and express your main idea. After you write your introduction, use your organized prewriting notes as a guide but depart from those notes when a good idea occurs to you. Write quickly. Do not worry about spelling or phrasing. You will have the opportunity to go back and fix such problems when you revise. Stop frequently and read what you have written. This practice will help you move logically from one thought to the next. Do not be afraid to return to the prewriting stage if you need more ideas or need to clarify your thinking. You can always stop and freewrite, brainstorm, or cluster to collect ideas. Write a conclusion that drives home the point of the composition. (Senn and Skinner 1995, 27)

Young writers need to realize that even a professional writer creates several drafts of a piece and then later revises, edits, and polishes it into a final work. Getting students to revise their writing is often difficult, and they must be taught the steps involved.

Some teachers refer to a first draft as a "sloppy copy" to legitimize the lack of concern and attention to the mechanics of writing that are needed at this phase to focus on content. It is sometimes recommended that when writing their rough drafts, students skip lines to allow room for later changes and revisions. If possible, teachers should allow students to create their rough drafts on computers. Research has shown that when students write on computers, they tend to write six times as much as they would if they wrote by hand. The reason for this is obvious. A computer eliminates the drudgery associated with writing because it can easily check for and correct misspelled words, indicate

FTCE Tip

A "sloppy copy" has great value.

potential grammatical errors, and allow the writer to insert and delete with ease as well as to completely rearrange a work, using cut and paste, without the need to rewrite the entire piece. If students use computers to construct their first drafts, then the later tasks of revising, editing, proofreading, and finally publishing their work will be greatly simplified.

Teachers are encouraged to conduct brief, informal conferences with students as they work on their rough drafts. In this way, they make themselves available to answer questions and provide encouragement. Comments should be as positive as possible. One technique is to use the "sandwich method" when and if it is necessary to offer constructive criticism: any comment that might be construed as negative is sandwiched between two positive remarks, so the overall impression is positive.

To learn to effectively revise their rough drafts, students should first read their work to themselves (some of them will profit from reading their writing aloud to themselves so that they can see and hear their work at the same time) and then read their drafts to one or more peers (after the class has been taught to provide useful, constructive criticism) and seek their comments and suggestions. In addition, students should look for anything in their writing that is unclear or does not communicate ideas effectively.

Revising

The third phase of the writing process is the revision of the first draft. Once again, it is important that students understand the importance of this aspect of the process, because many will consider themselves to be finished with the assigned writing as soon as they complete their rough drafts. Through repeated experiences with the entire writing process—particularly if they have opportunities to compare their rough drafts with revised, edited, and published pieces—they will begin to see how their writing emerges, changes, and improves from the beginning to the end.

At this point in the process, students should be considering adding ideas to their piece, adding details and information, rearranging elements of the piece to make it flow smoothly and logically, deleting unnecessary words, enriching the vocabulary by changing words or ideas that may not express what they want to say as clearly as they want to say it, and possibly using a revision checklist to keep track of revisions they made and to indicate additional revisions they may still want to make. A revision checklist might include the following:

Did you clearly state your main idea? Does your composition have a strong introduction, body, and conclusion? Did you support your main idea with enough details? Did you present your ideas in a logical order? Do any of your sentences stray from the main idea? Are your ideas clearly explained? Are your words specific? Are any words or ideas repeated unnecessarily? Are your sentences varied and smoothly connected? Is the purpose of your composition clear? (Senn and Skinner 1995, 31)

In providing instruction in revision, many teachers find it helpful to put an unrevised rough draft on a transparency and show it to the class on an overhead projector or to show it using a document camera projection system if that is available. The teacher should work with students to review the piece and make appropriate revisions, comparing the original with the revision to enable students to see the improvements as they emerge.

Editing

The next stage in the writing process is editing the piece. "Editing for spelling, grammar, and punctuation is important in writing material that is easily understood by others" (Roe and Ross 2006, 322). Some teachers provide their students with an editing checklist that includes the most common errors that writers make. These would include problems associated with grammar, punctuation, usage, spelling, and capitalization. Common questions frequently included on an editing checklist include the following:

Are your sentences completely free of errors in grammar and usage? Did you spell each word correctly? Did you use capital letters where needed? Did you punctuate each sentence correctly? Did you indent paragraphs as needed and leave proper margins on each side of the paper? (Senn and Skinner 1995, 35)

Each student can construct a personal editing checklist by recording examples of the kinds of errors that frequently occur in their writing along with the page in their English text that addresses that problem and examples of the corrected problem. The checklist then becomes a resource to be used for all future writing activities.

Proofreading

In the next phase of the writing process, students proofread their work and make corrections. Teach students common proofreading symbols such as ^ (insert), ¶ (start a new paragraph), ≡ (capital letter), and so forth. Most dictionaries include lists of proofreading symbols. Once they have learned the symbols, students can use them when editing their own writing, and the teacher can use proofreading symbols to correct student papers quickly and efficiently with confidence that students will understand their meaning. Students should keep a chart containing these symbols and what each represents in their writing folder for easy access and reference.

Publishing

The last phase of the writing process is publishing. This necessitates presenting the writing in final form and sharing it with the target audience. Students need to make a final copy of their writing in which they incorporate all the revisions and corrections indicated in earlier phases. Some ways in which students' work can be published at the school level include displaying the final work on a bulletin board in the classroom or in the school library; having students read their work to their classmates; collecting student work and adding it to a class collection in folders organized according to categories of writing; creating an anthology of students' work and sharing it with other classes; selecting a student's work to be submitted to a schoolwide publication, such as the school newspaper, yearbook, or literary magazine. A teacher interested in having students' work published beyond the school level can encourage them to submit pieces to newspapers or magazines; they can share their writing with an appropriate community group; or students can enter their work in writing contests.

EFFECTIVE RESPONSES TO STUDENTS' WRITING

The key to making responses to students' writing effective is giving students an opportunity to reflect on what they liked about their writing as well as on those things that still need attention. Comments of a general kind, such as "Good work" are ineffective because they are impersonal, fail to specify the "good" points of the writing, and do nothing to help writers focus on what they could do to improve their work.

Constructive criticism from both teachers and peers is most effective in responding to students' writing. To students, positive reinforcement of what they did well is more encouraging than attention called to what still needs work. When reviewing students' writing with them, the teacher can ask students what they liked best about their work. The teacher should focus on the level of success students have demonstrated in clearly expressing their purpose in writing their pieces. To guide students in addressing the issue of clarity, the teacher can challenge them to find places in their work that would benefit from clarification. Ask students to determine how successfully they addressed the intended audience and how they could improve this aspect of their writing. Finally, students can analyze their pieces to decide how effectively they maintain the reader's interest. Overall, the emphasis of constructive criticism is on the positive aspects of the writing and in guiding students' assessments of their own work.

METHODS TO ASSESS STUDENTS' WRITING

Every language arts or writing teacher should have a repertoire of methods available to assess students' writing. Different approaches work well for different students and for different types of writing. Some ways of appraising writing include conducting writing conferences either between the teacher and the student or between the student and his or her peers; using checklists to indicate the behaviors in which the student engages during each phase of the writing process; constructing and using a variety of forms specifically designed to record and evaluate progress in producing high-quality writing; and as mentioned earlier, portfolios, which provide authentic assessment and use actual examples of students' writing to document progress toward improvement. In addition, students can use individual tracking sheets, which are logs of students' writing, indicating the date, genre, format, status (prewriting, first draft, revising, editing, final copy), and comments about the progress of the piece. Some teachers have their students use writing comment sheets. While similar to individual tracking sheets, these forms include space for the teacher's comments on each piece of students' writing. Here are examples of an individual tracking sheet and a writing comment sheet:

Individual Writing Tracking Sheet

F = First Draft

R = Revising/Editing

FD = Final Draft

Name: _____

Date	Format	Status	Comments*

*Adapted from Oglan (2003, 101).

Writing Comment Sheet

Name: _____

Format	Date	Student's Comments	Teacher's Comments

References

Macmillan English: Thinking and writing processes, Teacher's ed. 1998. New York: Scribner Laidlaw.

Oglan, G. R. 2003. *Write, Right, Rite!* Boston: Allyn & Bacon.

Roe, B. C. and Ross, E. P. 2006. *Integrating language arts through literature & thematic units.* Boston: Allyn & Bacon.

Senn, J. A. and Skinner, C. A. 1995. *Heath English: An integrated approach to writing, Teacher's ed.* Lexington, MA: D. C. Heath & Co.

CHAPTER

The Use of the Reading Process to Construct Meaning from a Wide Range of Selections

TECHNIQUES FOR TEACHING STUDENTS TO UNDERSTAND ORGANIZATIONAL STRUCTURES OF LITERARY AND INFORMATIONAL MATERIAL

Expose youngsters to a variety of literary genres so that they may benefit from the different contributions that each offers. Each genre may be analyzed to understand how it is organized and how that particular organizational scheme suites the field. For example, each genre consists of organized literary elements such as plot, theme, characterization, setting, style, and point of view. In a novel or a short story, these elements inform the reader of the storyline, the message the story tries to convey, the people or animals about whom the story revolves, where and when the action takes place, how words and sentences are strung together, and finally, who is telling the story and the perspective used. Other specific genre that students need to study include historical fiction, contemporary realistic fiction, traditional literature, modern fantasy, science fiction, biography, autobiography, poetry, and various types of informational books.

The best way to teach students to understand the organizational structures of these materials is to expose them to several examples of each genre and to analyze the organization of each. Students can construct organizational outlines of the works that represent each genre and compare them to each other for commonalities. Another way for youngsters to become more aware of the organization of a particular genre is to put each element into a graphic organizer, such as a semantic web, and specify how each piece of literature addresses each element. For example, in the novel *The Great Gatsby,* by F. Scott Fitzgerald, the action is set on Long Island, New York. This is important to the plot because the reader is brought into the elegant lifestyle of the characters and is helped to understand Gatsby's lifelong yearning for wealth. By contrast, in the novel *Gone with the Wind,* Margaret Mitchell sets the story in several Georgia locations, Tara (Scarlett O'Hara's ancestral home), Twelve Oaks (Ashley's family estate), and Atlanta. Again, this setting is vital to the plot. This novel takes place shortly before, during, and after the American Civil War. Therefore, setting the novel in Georgia makes perfect sense as the story is told from the point of view of the Deep South. Students can discuss the setting of both of these books in order to understand each author's choice of setting. Once this has been done, the organizational structure of each type of writing will become more readily apparent.

> **FTCE Tip**
>
> Use graphic organizers to help students understand literary structures.

EFFECTIVE STRATEGIES TO ANALYZE TEXT

Context Clues

One strategy that youngsters need to learn to help them to analyze text is to use context clues. Briefly, the context of a word is "the surrounding words, or the situation in which the word is used. Generally the context of a word gives clues to that word's meaning rather than an outright definition" (Senn & Skinner, 1995, 449).

Restatement

Divide context clues into types and teach them in different categories. Sometimes a word in a sentence is used and then its meaning is restated in simpler terms that the reader is more likely to understand. For example, "The mayor had the support of the press in his *quest* for reform—this is his search for ways to govern the city better. [*Search* is a restatement of *quest.* This restatement helps to define *quest* as "an act of seeking: a pursuit."]

Example

Another category of context clues is that of giving an example. A word appears in a sentence and provides the context clue by way of an example of what the word means. Senn and Skinner give the following illustration: "Mr. Agarwal spoke about *celestial* matters; I remember best his vivid description of the Milky Way. [By using the description of the Milky Way as an example, the writer makes clear the meaning of *celestial*—"relating to the sky or the heavens."] (1995, 449).

Comparison

A third category of context clues is comparison. The writer includes a statement that compares the difficult word to something more familiar, and by doing so, helps the reader to define the unknown word. An example of this type of context clue is, "Joan Freitas recently completed her *memoirs,* a work rather like Agatha Christie's autobiography," she says. [The quotation helps to define *memoirs* as "a kind of autobiography" by making a comparison between Ms. Freitas's writing and Agatha Christie's autobiography.] (1995, 449).

Contrast

Another type of context clue is contrast. The author uses an unusual and perhaps unknown word but accompanies it with its antonym, a better known word. By doing this, the author has helped the reader to understand the more unusual word. Senn and Skinner provide the following instance: "Although the game seemed *frivolous* to me, the children played it with great seriousness." [The word *although* signals a contrast between the seriousness of the children and the seemingly *frivolous* game they were playing, suggesting that *frivolous* means "lacking in seriousness."] (1995, 449).

Parallelism

Finally, the last sort of context clue is parallelism. A case in point is the following: "She will *interrogate* the suspect; I will question the witness. [The parallel construction is a clue—but only a clue—that *interrogate* means "to question."] (1995, 449).

Word Structure

Another strategy that assists with text analysis is word structure. A reader who wishes to enrich and enlarge his vocabulary does so by reading extensively and widely. However, most of today's youngsters do not engage in very much reading; they read only what is required for school, textbooks, and perhaps an occasional novel in an English class or for a book report. Therefore, they are not exposed to unknown words with the repetition necessary for them to learn what they mean and to have those words become a part of their personal vocabulary. It is neither feasible nor productive to require students to memorize lists of individual words. Even if teachers make this a requirement, words learned in this manner will, at best, be stored in short-term rather than long-term memory. When encountering a word "learned" in this manner in a passage, students may recognize that they have seen it before, but they will not remember what it means. A more efficient approach is to teach students to focus on word parts such as prefixes and base words. Once students know the meanings of a large number of prefixes and base words, they can apply this knowledge to the analysis of unknown words and meet with a great deal of success in determining their meaning. Knowledge of suffixes usually helps to decide into what part of speech the words fall. Lists of common and useful prefixes, base words, and suffixes are readily available in most English texts. Students should learn the meanings of these and get practice in determining what words containing these prefixes, base words, and suffixes mean.

Analogies

Knowledge of synonyms and antonyms assists students in expanding their vocabulary. Teach students to use a thesaurus in hard copy or on a computer to find an antonym or synonym for words they are learning. This sort of knowledge will reinforce their knowledge of words and help them remember the meanings of many words.

Structure

Strategies for text analysis also include recognizing analogies. This requires the analysis of the relationship between the two words originally presented so that two other words that share the same relationship can be correctly chosen as analogous. Students need to be taught that words can be analogous because they are synonyms, antonyms, express a part/whole relationship, demonstrate a worker/tool relationship, show a worker and his/her product, an object and its purpose or use, and the like. Once students learn these categories of analogous relationships, they will find it easier to identify the correct answer. Knowledge of analogous relationships extends the students' vocabulary and aids comprehension.

An additional strategy to aid students in analyzing text is to recognize the structure of what they are reading. Some organizational structures embrace the following: comparing and contrasting, incorporating a description, providing a sequence, analyzing cause and effect, and providing a problem and its solution (Roe & Ross, 2006). Teachers should provide books that exemplify these different organizational patterns and provide practice for their students in identifying them.

TECHNIQUES FOR TEACHING STUDENTS THE USES OF A WIDE VARIETY OF REFERENCE MATERIALS

Many reference works are immensely helpful in many aspects of language arts. Teachers cannot assume that their students are familiar with all of them or that they know how to make the best use of them. Direct instruction is necessary.

Dictionary

The most widely used reference work is the dictionary. Students are usually exposed to this aid early in elementary school, yet most of them fail to use it correctly. Just like several other reference books, it is organized alphabetically and provides not only the meaning or more often the several meanings of words, but it also tells the word's origin, its correct spelling, its correct pronunciation, synonyms, antonyms, and the part of speech. Some dictionaries, particularly those intended for younger users, provide a sentence in which the word of choice is used correctly. The main feature of a dictionary that students seem to disregard is the guidewords. These words, at the top of each page, tell the students the first and last words on each page. Users ignore this help and look at each word in a

FTCE Tip

Have students practice using guidewords!

hunt for the word they are seeking to define. Eventually, they are able to locate their target word but they have wasted a lot of time in the process. Give students practice in using a dictionary to define words, to note their origins, to spell them correctly, and to get help in correctly using the words in sentences. Watch closely to see how they find the words and correct them if they fail to use the guidewords. Try giving them a very short time limit in which to locate words, thus forcing them to use guidewords for efficiency.

Encyclopedia

An encyclopedia is another reference work that teachers must show their students how to use correctly. Like a dictionary, entries in an encyclopedia are arranged alphabetically. Entries in an encyclopedia are listed by topic and provide a broad overview of a topic. As such, articles in encyclopedias are often a good starting point for research on a topic, particularly on a subject that students know little about at the start of the assignment. There are a number of encyclopedias available and teachers should identify those most appropriate for the reading level and experience of the students. In addition to general encyclopedias, you should also acquaint your students with specialized encyclopedias such as those dedicated to art (*Encyclopedia of Modern Art*) or to animals (*Encyclopedia of Animal Care*).

Who's Who

If students need to locate information about a particular person, other references for that purpose include *Who's Who, Current Biography,* and *Webster's Biographical Dictionary.* As with other types of references, you need to teach your students the purposes and uses of each. Assign reports on individuals, living and dead. Include specific questions that the students are required to answer. If necessary, acquaint them with specialized resources such as *British Authors of the Nineteenth Century* or *Contemporary Authors.*

Atlas

You need to teach youngsters how to use atlases to locate maps and to get information related to the geography of the places of interest. Some useful atlases for this purpose include *Goode's World Atlas* and the *National Geographic Atlas of the World.* Challenge students to locate specific information about regions of the world, a specific country, a particular body of water, and the like. Some students may head for an encyclopedia to retrieve needed information. This would be an ideal opportunity to direct them to an atlas as a more relevant resource.

Readers' Guide to Periodical Literature

Another reference work that students should learn about is the *The Readers' Guide to Periodical Literature.* This is "an index to articles published in 180 periodicals throughout the United States and Canada. It is a useful source for tracking down articles in news magazines like *Time* and *Newsweek* and other general-interest magazines, such as *Business Week* and *Glamour*" (*Macmillan English*, 1988, 725). Assignments that require students to locate information for general public consumption will teach them the use of this guide.

Almanacs

You should also familiarize your students with almanacs, sometimes called yearbooks, which are appropriate for locating facts in many categories, such as sports, entertainment, science, history, current events, geography, and the arts. Assignments requiring information of a factual nature would necessitate the use of an almanac and serve to acquaint students with this specialized resource.

STRATEGIES TO DEVELOP AND ENHANCE READING COMPREHENSION

Without comprehension, true reading does not exist. Decoding words without putting meaning to them is a futile activity. Therefore, teachers must employ a variety of strategies to initially develop and then to enhance reading comprehension.

Reading Strategies

Schema Theory

One aspect of reading comprehension is the use of reading strategies. One such strategy is schema theory. This involves the use of stored clusters of concepts based on prior knowledge. Each of these stored clusters is called a schema, and readers apply them as they read to make sense of text. Schemas are modified in relation to what is gained as they read the current text. According to the National Read Panel (2000), "when readers actively relate their own knowledge and experiences to ideas in the text, their comprehension improves" (Roe & Ross 2006, 248). Obviously, students who lack rich experiences are at a disadvantage in trying to use prior knowledge to relate to and to make sense of text. Therefore, teachers need to build students' experiences through direct or vicarious encounters.

Metacognition

Another characteristic of enhanced reading comprehension is metacognition. This is defined as, "The ability to understand and control one's own thought processes. . ." (Roe & Ross 2006, 249). Students who possess this characteristic "realize what they know and what they don't know, set purposes, select appropriate reading and learning strategies, monitor (check) their understanding, and evaluate their performance" (Roe & Ross 2006, 249). Teachers need to emphasize metacognition by encouraging their students to relate text to prior knowledge, make predictions, ask questions while reading, construct images or visualize while reading, and to summarize what they have read. Readers who use metacognition also use rereading to clarify text they find confusing the first time they read it. Model metacognitive strategies for students and have them practice each of them as they read so that they become routine.

Reciprocal Reading

Reciprocal reading is another strategy used to increase comprehension. There are four parts to reciprocal reading: predicting, generating questions, clarifying, and summarizing. In order to predict, students have to anticipate what will happen next. Generating questions refers to asking questions based on information in the text combined with background knowledge. Clarifying is the process of identifying those parts of the text that the student finds confusing and attempting to eliminate the confusion. Finally, summarizing refers to putting together the most important ideas expressed in the text (Roe & Ross 2006). This strategy is termed reciprocal because the students and the teacher take turns playing the role of teacher. As the teacher, you model each step in the process at first and gradually turn it over to the students, whom you continue to guide as they employ each step in the process.

Fluency

Fluency is also vital to reading comprehension. Defined, fluency is "the ability to project the natural pitch, stress, and juncture of the spoken word on written text, automatically and at a natural rate" (Roe & Ross 2006, 260-61). When readers possess fluency, they identify and decode words rapidly, and automatically make inferences, thus they are free to focus on comprehension. Methods for promoting fluency include modeling by having a fluent reader read aloud. The students should follow the text as it is read and either repeat the text or read along. A second method includes repeated readings. This requires students to read and reread the same text many times. The students can practice this independently or read along with a tape of the text. A third strategy to improve fluency is the use of paired oral readings. Two students each read the same passage silently. They then take turns reading the passage three times orally in succession to their partners. The partners respond by giving suggestions and positive feedback to their partners. The use of an oral recitation lesson is another way to improve fluency. In this approach, the teacher selects text and models fluent reading. After the passage is read, a comprehension strategy is discussed. Students practice reading as a group and individually. Finally, they read a portion of the text for an audience as a performance.

FTCE Tip

Positive feedback in paired oral reading improves fluency.

Choral Reading

Choral reading is another strategy used to improve fluency. "Poetry is often used for choral reading. It can be read in unison, one line per child, cumulatively, or in groups" (Roe

& Ross 2006, 263). Lastly, teachers can use Reader's Theater. In this approach, students practice reading aloud expressively from a script and then perform for an audience.

METHODS OF ASSESSING STUDENTS' READING PROGRESS TO DETERMINE STRENGTHS AND WEAKNESSES

Assessment methods include informal procedures that may consist of daily observation (the most widely used method), checklists, rubrics, for inclusion in a portfolio, running records, and informal reading inventories. In addition, there are any number of standardized tests to assess reading and to define specific strengths and weaknesses.

Assessment Methods

Daily Observation

Skilled teachers can use daily observation to gather data to record on checklists, rubrics, running records, and informal reading inventories.

Checklist

A checklist is easily and quickly constructed and can be used to record dichotomous data indicating on a yes/no basis what a student is capable or incapable of doing. Some checklists combine a rating scale with the checklist. When categories on this type of checklist are evaluated, a numerical or letter rating is given to each item. In this way, not only is the presence or absence of a characteristic indicated, but the degree to which it is present is shown as well. Items such as the following might typically appear on a reading checklist: uses prior knowledge, makes reasonable predictions, uses context clues to construct meaning, uses word structure to construct meaning, uses metacognition to monitor reading, chooses books at an appropriate reading level, and reads a variety of genres (Bromley 1992)

Rubric

A rubric is defined as a form that "enables the user to rate the quality of student performance according to a predetermined set of criteria and standards" (Roe & Ross 2006, 520). Usually, rubrics have a rating scale in which the biggest number represents the best score. A rubric to evaluate reading might be similar to the following:

Criteria	3	2	1
Blends	Uses blends consistently	Uses blends inconsistently	Has difficulty blending
Punctuation	Uses voice inflection to reflect written punctuation	Attends to some types of punctuation	Reads through punctuation
Sight Words	Recognizes most	Recognizes some	Fails to recognize
Word Structure	Uses to derive meaning	Sometimes uses to derive meaning	Fails to use to derive meaning
Main Idea	Consistently able to identify	Usually able to identify	Usually unable to identify
Inference	Able to draw from most text	Able to draw from some text	Usually unable to draw from text
Vocabulary	Knows meaning of most words encountered	Knows meaning of many words encountered	Does not know meaning of most words encountered
Total			

Running Record

A running record documents a child's reading as he/she reads out loud. This type of assessment allows you to evaluate the reading level as well as to note explicit types of miscues. Specific marks are used to indicate the kinds of errors the reader made, such as substitutions, omissions, insertions, self-corrections, and so on. You need some training to use this form of assessment, but with practice, it can be done quickly and easily.

Informal Reading Inventory

An Informal Reading Inventory is very similar to a reading record in that for part of the assessment, the student reads aloud, and the teacher uses symbols to note the types of miscues the student makes. However, this tool differs from a running record in that the student reads graded passages and then responds to comprehension questions specifically designed to detect the ability to grasp the main idea of the passage, to use inference to draw conclusions, to remember details, and to understand vocabulary. For the second part of this assessment, the student reads the passages silently and then responds to comprehension questions. The amount of time it takes for the youngster to read the passage is also noted.

Diagnosis of Errors

Searching for patterns of errors can help teachers to diagnose weaknesses as well as strengths. Noting specific types of errors leads to detecting certain weaknesses such as that made by a student who misreads a word because he reads without regard for meaning, and that made by another student who may misread a word by substituting a synonym without regard for the visual appearance of the word. As a teacher, your attempts to remediate this difficulty would differ with the student, as even though both misread the same word, the causes of the miscue are completely different. Therefore, diagnosis of specific errors leads to targeted remediation that is far more likely to be successful than general correction.

References

Bromley, K. D. 1992. *Language arts: Exploring connections.* Upper Saddle River, NJ: Prentice Hall.

Macmillan English: Thinking and writing processes, Teacher's ed. 1988. New York: Scribner Laidlaw.

Roe, B. C. and Ross, E. P. 2006. *Integrating language arts through literature & thematic units.* Boston: Allyn & Bacon.

Senn, J. A. and Skinner, C. A. 1995. *Health English: An integrated approach to writing, Teacher's ed.* Lexington, MA: D. C. Heath & Co.

Knowledge of Literature and Methods for Effective Teaching

5

LITERARY DEVICES IN FICTION AND NONFICTION

Works of fiction and nonfiction typically use literary devices, such as those related to sound: alliteration, assonance, onomatopoeia, rhyme, and rhythm. Other authors use devices employing figurative language, such as imagery, metaphor, and simile.

Literary Devices

Alliteration

Alliteration is the repetition of the same consonant sound at the beginning of several successive words. An example of alliteration is the tongue twister "Peter Piper picked a peck of pickled peppers." Assonance is the repetition of a vowel sound within words. Here is an example from Edgar Allan Poe's "The Bells": "From the molten-golden notes." Onomatopoeia is the use of words whose sounds suggest their meaning. Examples of this literary device are *hum, plop, fizz, click, splash, moo,* and *thump.* Rhyme refers to "the repetition of accented syllables with the same vowel and consonant sounds" (Senn and Skinner 1995, 398). An example of rhyme is this excerpt from "Stopping by Woods on a Snowy Evening" by Robert Frost:

The woods are lovely, dark, and deep,
But I have promises to keep,
And miles to go before I sleep

Rhythm

Rhythm is the distinct beat produced by a pattern of accented and unaccented syllables. In the following selection from Emily Dickinson's "Because I could not stop for Death," each accented syllable is indicated by an accent mark over the letter (á) and each unaccented syllable by a carat (â):

Bêcaúse Î coúld nôt stóp fôr Deáth—
Hê kińdly stopped fôr mé

Imagery

Imagery is the "use of concrete details to create a picture or appeal to senses other than sight" (Senn and Skinner 1995, 400). An example of the use of this device is the following from "Recuerdo" by Edna St. Vincent Millay:

And the sky went wan, and the wind came cold,
And the sun rose dripping, a bucketful of gold.

Metaphor and simile are other literary devices, both of which were defined and discussed in Chapter 3.

CHARACTERISTICS OF VARIOUS LITERARY GENRES, MOVEMENTS, AND CRITICAL APPROACHES

Each of the many literary genres has a specific set of attributes that help to define it. Among the genres frequently used with children and young people are folk literature, fantasy literature, realistic fiction, nonfiction, and poetry.

Folk Literature

Included under the category of folk literature are nursery rhymes, ballads, epics, myths, legends, tall tales, folktales, fairy tales, and animal tales. Mother Goose and nursery rhymes, ballads, and epics are included in the subgenre of poetry. Subgenres of prose are myths, legends, tall tales, folktales, fairy tales, and fables.

Nursery Rhymes

Mother Goose and nursery rhymes include "anonymous jingles, riddles, chants, verses, and songs in couplets, quatrains, and limericks" (Goforth 1998, 72). These have long served to amuse and entertain young children as they recite them and listen to them. The rhymes often tell the fantastical adventures of humans or animals. Typically, the themes of nursery rhymes include the basic concerns of childhood, like love, hope, and security. In nursery rhymes, the plots consist of imaginary adventures and are often illogical. The characters can be animate or inanimate, adults or children. Sometimes magical animals or objects appear in nursery rhymes. As a rule, nursery rhymes are easy to remember (some are tongue twisters) and have characters that appeal to young children. Nursery rhymes are used for learning the alphabet, numbers, and counting aloud.

Ballads

Ballads are short songs that exalt the deeds and adventures of either ordinary people or celebrated heroes. Historically, ballads were used to entertain royalty, were often accompanied by instruments, and served as dance music. The themes of ballads celebrate the virtues and personality of the hero and include courage, valor, patriotism, death, romance, and tragedy. The plot revolves around a short adventure, typically a single incident or moment in the hero's life. The characters may be real or legendary. Ballads are set in an actual place at a real time. The words of the ballad are far more important than its music.

Epics

An epic is a "long narrative, written in grandiose language, relating heroic deeds of an historical/regional hero; [it] represents national values and culture" in an authentic setting (Goforth 1998, 72). The theme of an epic deals with virtues and feats valued by a society; these include physical strength, patience, and wisdom. The plot of an epic is a long narrative, episodic, and often includes a quest. The characters in an epic are frequently national heroes or superhuman. The main character often accomplishes impossible tasks with the help of gods or superhuman beings. The hero usually must struggle with evil forces. The setting of an epic is an ancient, unknown time, in a real place. Examples of epics include *Beowulf, The Iliad,* and *Paradise Lost.*

Myths

"Myths are anonymous, symbolic stories presented as having occurred in a previous age; they explain supernatural traditions of a people, their gods, heroes, cultural traits, beliefs, and natural phenomena" (Goforth 1998, 79). The plots of myths are often complex and concern conflicts between gods and humans. The characters in myths are gods and goddesses who have human strengths and weaknesses. They often represent certain abstract values. Myths are usually set in prehistoric times or in an imaginary world.

Legends

Legends are "exaggerated tales told as fact by one in the 'know' about real places, people, and events; the teller embellishes the facts to make the character 'bigger-than-life'" (Goforth 1998, 79). In a legend, the personality, deeds, goals, and beliefs of the hero are represented. The tale is told in episodes, and the story tends to get more exaggerated each time it is told. The plot is focused on one major event in the hero's life, an "extraordinary historical event, or why a natural phenomenon exists" (82). The characters in legends are based on either real persons or combinations of actual persons. Gods are not included in legends, but real and fictional people and animals are. Supposedly, a person who knows the "true story" tells the legend. The setting of a legend is defined and identified with a real person and real events.

Tall Tales

Tall tales concern a "boisterous, extraordinary character endowed with physical prowess" (Goforth 1998, 79) and may be loosely based on and assimilate the beliefs, values, and mores of a society" (4). The theme of a tall tale is an issue of concern to ordinary people, such as "survival, human behavior, and human interaction with other humans, animals, places, and events" (84). What makes a tall tale "tall" is the exaggerated nature of the events.

Folktales

Folktales are "short fictionalized prose narratives that are not historically accurate, but authentically represent the culture, region, or ethnic group that created them" (Goforth 1998, 85). Characteristically, the theme of a folktale involves human dreams, wishes, and fantasies. The plot of a folktale is simple and linear. The story is formulaic and has a beginning, three events, and a quick conclusion. Folktales are action packed and have timeless or unknown characters who typically have supernatural or magical powers. The names of the characters and their manner of speaking reflect the culture. The story contains figurative, descriptive, and repetitive language with predictable phrases and words.

Fantasy

Fantasy literature consists of "imaginary verbal and visual narratives that evoke wonder and magic impossible in the real world" (Goforth 1998, 4). There are four subgenres of fantasy literature: fairy tales, low fantasy, high fantasy, and science fiction.

- Literary fairy tales focus on universal concerns. Typically, humility wins out over wealth. Simple logic triumphs over the educated youth. The format consists of three incidents or episodes and there is a logical structure, suspenseful adventure, simple events, plausible occurrences, and usually a happy conclusion. The characters are believable and often idealistic, ordinary people rather than royalty.

- Low fantasy "is characterized by book-length fanciful narratives set primarily in the real, primary world, but including characters or events with plausible fantasy elements. The term *low fantasy* refers to the setting—the primary world—and is not an indication of the importance assigned to the subgenre, nor is it used as an evaluative term" (Goforth 1998, 111).

- High fantasy "is characterized by imaginary book-length narratives set primarily in a 'secondary world'; the narratives are rooted in folk literature and epic in proportion. These fantasies are created from the fantasist's vision and imagination. The real and fanciful humans, animals, and creatures become involved in magical or supernatural experiences that defy reality" (Goforth 1998, 117).

Science Fiction

Science fiction is defined as an imaginative narrative that "deals with the reaction of human responses to changes in the level of science and technology" (Goforth 1998, 121). The theme of science fiction is often a fight between good and evil. The author is portraying his "perception of the impact of science and technology on the future development of society" (126). The characters in science fiction are often stereotyped, and the protagonist succeeds by relying on intellect rather than emotions. Often the characters start in the present and move to the future. Science fiction writers tend to produce series of books, and students who enjoy a particular author are apt to read every book in a series.

Fairy Tales

Fairy tales "are imaginary 'wonder tales' that include enchantments and supernatural or marvelous elements and occurrences. Magic charms, disguises, and spells are frequently used by supernatural characters to protect or help the human or animal characters" (Goforth 1998, 88). Fairy tales are concerned with the dreams, goals, and wishes of ordinary people. Invariably, good triumphs over evil and the poor over the rich. The focus is on a single hero who is frequently the youngest in the family and who completes three tasks to reach a goal. The characters in fairy tales are stereotypical and frequently do not have names. Sometimes they may be transformed into animals or even plants. Typically, fairy tales include spirits, demons, dragons, giants, and monsters. The language used in fairy tales is that of common people, and they often begin "Once upon a time" and end with "they lived happily ever after." The setting of a fairy tale is usually not defined but is a kind of never-never land.

Fables

Fables are "short animal tales intended to teach a lesson. Generally, the moral (or lesson) is stated at the end of the story. One animal clearly depicts good traits while another exhibits bad characteristics" (Goforth 1998, 95). A fable usually teaches a lesson about human nature and relationships; its plot is short and simple; and it ends with a stated moral. The characters in a fable are often talking animals that are not well developed and not very important to the story.

Movements in Literature

Over the course of history, there have been numerous movements in literature. Some of the better-known movements are romanticism, realism, symbolism, modernism, surrealism, and existentialism.

Romanticism

Romanticism flourished in the eighteenth and nineteenth centuries. It began in Germany and England and quickly spread throughout Europe. The movement spread to the Western Hemisphere and has made its presence known in musical form around the globe. Romanticism "emphasized imagination, fancy, and freedom, emotion, wildness, beauty of the natural world, the rights of the individual, the nobility of the common man, and the attractiveness of the pastoral life" (*Prentice Hall Literature* 1996, 1482). Writers representative of the Romantic Movement were William Wordsworth, Lord Byron, Percy Bysshe Shelley, and Victor Hugo.

Realism

Realism was a nineteenth-century reaction to romanticism. The form of literature that gained particular popularity at this time was the novel. Realism is the "true to life" approach to subject matter. Rejecting the classical themes common in literature like mythology and ballads, realists preferred to focus on everyday life. Writers who epitomized this movement include Balzac, Flaubert, George Eliot, Dostoevsky, and Tolstoy (*http://encyclopedia.thefreedictionary.com/Literary+realism*).

Symbolism

Symbolism was a literary movement that "reached its peak in the last two decades of the nineteenth century."

> It denotes an early modernist literary movement initiated in France during the nineteenth century that reacted against the prevailing standards of realism. Writers in this movement aimed to evoke, indirectly and symbolically, an order of being beyond the material world of the five senses. Poetic expression of personal emotion figured strongly in the movement, typically by means of a private set of symbols uniquely identifiable with the individual poet. The principal aim of the Symbolists was to express in words the highly complex feelings that grew out of everyday contact with the world. In a broader sense, the term 'symbolism refers to the use of one object to represent another. Early members of the Symbolist movement included the French authors Charles Baudelaire and Arthur Rimbaud; William Butler Yeats, James Joyce, and T. S. Eliot were influenced as the movement moved to Ireland, England, and the United States. Examples of the concept of symbolism include a flag that stands for a nation or movement, or an empty cupboard used to suggest hopelessness, poverty, and despair. (*www.answers.com/topic/symbolism?print=true*)

Modernism

Modernism is mostly associated with the first decades of the twentieth century. The term *modernist* can describe the content and the form of a work, or either aspect alone. Typical of modernism is experimentation and the realization that knowledge is not absolute. Common themes in modernist literature are the loss of a sense of tradition and the dominance of technology. Several theories put forth at the turn of the twentieth century influenced modernist writers, including Einstein's theory of relativity, Planck's quantum theory, and Freud's theories on the unconscious.

Surrealism

Surrealism is another literary movement; it began in the early 1920s. Works from this period feature the element of surprise, unexpected juxtapositions, and non sequitur. André Breton is considered the leader of this movement, which began in Paris and soon spread around the world. Surrealists aimed to free people from what they saw as false rationality and restrictive customs and structures. Breton proclaimed the true aim of surrealism is "long live the social revolution and it alone!" To this goal, at various times surrealists aligned with communism and anarchism. Surrealists thought to use Freud's free association work, dream analysis, and the unconscious to free imagination.

Existentialism

The existentialism movement emphasized individual existence, freedom, and choice and influenced writers in the nineteenth and twentieth centuries. The Danish philosopher Søren Kierkegaard, the first writer to refer to himself as an existentialist, stated, "the highest good for the individual is to find his or her own unique vocation" (*http://encarta.msn. com/text_761555530__-0/Existentialism.html*). Traditionalists argue that moral choice involves an objective judgment of right and wrong, while existentialists contend that there is no objective, rational basis for moral choice. In addition to Kierkegaard, other noted existentialist writers are Pascal, Nietzsche, Heidegger, and Sartre.

Literary Criticism

Literary criticism defines, classifies, analyzes, interprets, and evaluates works of literature. Types of literary criticism include the following:

- Historical criticism uses history to understand a literary work more clearly. It looks at the social and intellectual currents in which the author wrote.

- Textual criticism uses two main processes: recension and emendation. Recension is the selection, after thorough examination of all possible material, of only the most trustworthy evidence on which to base a text. Emendation is the effort to eliminate all the errors found in even the best manuscripts.

- Feminist criticism seeks to correct or to supplement what is regarded as a predominantly male-dominated critical perspective with a female consciousness. It attempts to understand literature from a woman's point of view.

- Biographical criticism uses knowledge of the author's life experiences to gain a better understanding of the writer's work.

- Cultural criticism focuses on the historical, social, and economic contexts of a work.

- Formal criticism pays particular attention to formal elements of the work, such as the language, structure, and tone. It analyzes form and meaning, paying special attention to diction, irony, paradox, metaphor, and symbols. It also examines plot, characterization, and narrative technique.

HOW ALLUSIONS FROM A VARIETY OF SOURCES CONTRIBUTE TO LITERATURE

Allusions are references to well-known persons, places, events, literary works, or works of art used to enrich literature. Allusions make connections and thereby provide a deeper meaning that helps to clarify the writer's intentions. For example, a character in a novel might say to a pretentious writer, "Who do you think you are, Shakespeare?" The reference to the world-renowned playwright would make the insult complete. Another character might wonder about the youthful appearance of a contemporary and might ask if she looked so young because she had a picture in the attic. This reference to *The Portrait of Dorian Gray,* by Oscar Wilde, clearly communicates to the reader that the inquisitive character wonders what means, devious or otherwise, the other person used to retain a youthful façade. Nowadays, when someone mentions 9/11 in a text, the reader can be sure that the reference is to the horrific events that took place on that date in 2001; it is not necessary to provide details because they are globally known.

FTCE Tip

Allusions help to make an author's meaning more clear.

MAJOR AUTHORS WHO REPRESENT THE DIVERSITY OF AMERICAN CULTURE

The following is a sampling of American authors who represent diversity. Works of these authors with their divergent viewpoints should be shared with students.

Edward Albee	Jack London
Louisa May Alcott	Norman Mailer
Maya Angelou	William Maxwell
James Baldwin	Herman Melville
Saul Bellow	Arthur Miller
Ray Bradbury	Henry Miller
Pearl S. Buck	Toni Morrison
Truman Capote	Joyce Carol Oates
Willa Cather	Clifford Odets
Raymond Chandler	Sylvia Plath
James Fenimore Cooper	Edgar Allan Poe
e. e. cummings	J. D. Salinger
Emily Dickinson	Sam Sheppard
Frederick Douglass	Upton Sinclair
W. E. B. DuBois	Susan Sontag
T. S. Eliot	Gertrude Stein
Ralph Ellison	John Steinbeck
Ralph Waldo Emerson	Robert Louis Stevenson
William Falkner	Henry David Thoreau
F. Scott Fitzgerald	Laura Tohe
Robert Frost	John Kennedy Toole
Nathaniel Hawthorne	Mark Twain
Abbie Hoffman	John Updike
Langston Hughes	Gore Vidal
Jack Kerouac	Edith Wharton
Harper Lee	Walt Whitman
Sinclair Lewis	Tennessee Williams

This list is not meant to be exhaustive, and teachers are not expected to become experts on all these authors. However, it would be worthwhile to review the major works of these authors and to have some familiarity with each.

PRINCIPAL PERIODS OF BRITISH LITERATURE AND AMERICAN LITERATURE, MAJOR AUTHORS, AND REPRESENTATIVE WORKS

Periods of British Literature, Major Authors, and Representative Works

450–1066: Old English (or Anglo-Saxon) Period

This period of literature spans from the invasion of Celtic England by the Germanic tribes in the first half of the fifth century to the Battle of Hastings and the conquest of England by William the Conqueror. Literature during this time developed from an oral tradition, and in the eighth century, poetry appeared. The epic poem *Beowulf* was written. Caedmon and Cynewulf were two poets of this period who wrote on biblical and religious themes.

1066–1500: Middle English Period

The literature of this period was written during the four and a half centuries between the Norman Conquest and 1500, at which point the language derived from the dialect of the London area became known as Modern English. The writings of this period have secular rather than religious themes, and the best known are *The Canterbury Tales* by Geoffrey Chaucer and *Sir Gawain and the Green Knight* by an unknown author.

1500–1660: The Renaissance

Writers prominent during the beginning of this period were Sir Thomas More and Sir Thomas Wyatt. The four subsets of this period are described in the following paragraphs.

1558–1603: **Elizabethan Age**	The Elizabethan Age coincides with the reign of Elizabeth I. The literature of this time reflects medieval tradition and the optimism of the Renaissance. The major styles of literature of this period are lyric poetry, prose, and drama. Among the major writers of the time are William Shakespeare, Christopher Marlowe, Edmund Spenser, Sir Walter Raleigh, and Ben Johnson.
1603–1625: **Jacobean Age**	The Jacobean Age coincides with the reign of James I. The literature became more sophisticated and full of rivalry during this period. Works produced include the King James Bible and the poetry and prose of John Donne, Francis Bacon, and Thomas Middleton.
1625–1649: **Caroline Age**	The Caroline Age coincides with the reign of Charles I. This age produced a group of poets known as the Cavalier Poets, and the dramatists of this period were the last to write in the Elizabethan tradition.
1649–1660: **Commonwealth Period**	The Commonwealth Period (also known as the Puritan Interregnum) includes the literature written during the time Oliver Cromwell ruled England. Major writers of the period include John Milton, Thomas Hobbes, and Andrew Marvell. In 1642, the Puritans closed the theaters on moral and religious grounds. The theaters remained closed for 18 years.

1660–1785: Neoclassical Period

This period was heavily influenced by the French literature of the day. Literature of this time is known for its use of philosophy, reason, skepticism, wit, and refinement. The three subsets of this period are described in the following paragraphs.

1660–1700: **Restoration**	The Restoration is so called because it was the time during which the monarchy was restored and reason and tolerance triumphed over religious and political passion. Writers of this period produced prose, poetry, and comedy. Milton wrote *Paradise Lost* and *Paradise Regained* during this period. Other major authors are John Dryden and John Locke.

1700–1745: Augustan Age (or Age of Pope)	The Augustan Age featured the works of Jonathan Swift, Alexander Pope, and Daniel Defoe. The characteristics of the writings of this time are refinement, clarity, elegance, and balanced judgment.
1745–1785: Age of Sensibility (or Age of Johnson)	During the Age of Sensibility, literature began to emphasize instinct and feeling rather than judgment and restraint. Interest in medieval ballads and folk literature arose at this time. Another name for the period is the Age of Johnson, because Samuel Johnson and those in his literary circle were prominent authors. In addition, great early novels such as *Clarissa* (1748) by Samuel Richardson and Henry Fielding's *Tom Jones* (1749) were written during this time.

1785–1830: Romantic Period

The literature of this time is very personal in nature, frequently uses symbolism, and explores nature and the supernatural. Well-known writers of this time are Samuel Taylor Coleridge, William Wordsworth, Jane Austen, and Lord Byron. Gothic literature also began during this time. This literature takes place in dark and gloomy settings and includes characters and incidences that are fantastic, grotesque, savage, mysterious, and frequently melodramatic. Two of the most well-known Gothic novelists are Anne Radcliffe and Mary Shelley.

1832–1901: Victorian Period

This period began when Victoria assumed the throne in 1837 and ended with her death in 1901. Literature of the period deals with contemporary issues as well as problems surrounding the Industrial Revolution, class tensions, the early feminist movement, issues of political and social reform, and the impact of Charles Darwin's theory of evolution. Some of the most prominent authors of the time are Alfred Lord Tennyson, Elizabeth Barrett Browning, Robert Browning, Matthew Arnold, Charles Dickens, Charlotte Brontë, George Eliot, and Thomas Hardy. The two literary movements that occurred during the Victorian Period are the Pre-Raphaelites and the movement of Aestheticism and Decadence.

1848–1860: **Pre-Raphaelites**	In 1848, a group of English artists formed the Pre-Raphaelite Brotherhood. The group took the truthfulness, simplicity, and religious devotion that existed in painting before Raphael and the Italian Renaissance and incorporated them into their writing. The outcome of this blending was the Pre-Raphaelites.
1880–1900: **Aestheticism and Decadence Movement**	The Aestheticism and Decadence Movement of English literature was an outgrowth of the French movement of the same name. Authors of the period encouraged experimentation and held the view that art is totally opposed to "natural" norms of morality. Writers of the time opposed the domination of scientific thinking. From this movement, the phrase *art for art's sake* emerged. Oscar Wilde is a well-known author of the period.

1901–1914: Edwardian Period

This period was named for King Edward VII and lasted from Queen Victoria's death to the beginning of World War I. The British Empire was at its height. While some people enjoyed great wealth and luxurious lifestyles, many others lived in overwhelming poverty. The authors of this period used their writing to comment on the prevailing social conditions. The social commentary of George Bernard Shaw and H. G. Wells attacks injustice and the insensitivity of the upper classes. Other outstanding writers of this period are William Butler Yeats, Joseph Conrad, Rudyard Kipling, Henry James, and E. M. Forster.

1910–1936: Georgian Period

This period is named for the reign of George V. Many writers of the Edwardian Period continued to write during this period. This era also produced a group of poets known as the Georgian poets. This poetry focuses on rural subject matter and is traditional in technique and form.

1914–1945: Modern Period

The literature in this period was written from the beginning of World War I (1914). Authors of this period experimented with subject matter, form, and style. Poets who wrote during this period include W. B. Yeats, T. S. Eliot, Dylan Thomas, and Seamus Heaney.

Among the novelists of the time are James Joyce, D. H. Lawrence, and Virginia Woolf. Playwrights include Noel Coward and Samuel Beckett.

1945–Present: Postmodern Period

This period followed World War II (1939–1945). It blends literary genres and styles in an attempt to be free of modernist forms.

Periods of American Literature, Major Authors, and Representative Works

1607–1776: Colonial Period

This period encompasses the first settlement in Jamestown to the beginning of the Revolution. The themes of the writings of this period are primarily religious, practical, or historical. The most influential writers of the period are John Winthrop, Cotton Mather, Benjamin Franklin, and Anne Bradstreet.

1765–1790: Revolutionary Age

This period is best known for the writing of some of the greatest documents in American history. In 1776, Thomas Paine wrote *Common Sense* and Thomas Jefferson wrote the Declaration of Independence. In 1781, the Articles of Confederation were ratified. *The Federalist Papers* were written by Alexander Hamilton, James Madison, and John Jay between 1787 and 1788. The Constitution of the United States was drafted in 1787 and ratified in 1789.

1775–1828: Early National Period

The writers of this period wrote in the English style, but the settings, themes, and characters are genuinely American. Some of the most recognized writers of this period are Washington Irving, James Fenimore Cooper, and Edgar Allan Poe.

1828–1865: Romantic Period (or American Renaissance)

The works of these writers helped shape the ideas, ideals, and literary aims of many American writers. Among the well-known writers of the period are Ralph Waldo

Emerson, Henry David Thoreau, Edgar Allan Poe, Herman Melville, Nathaniel Hawthorne, Harriet Beecher Stowe, Henry Wadsworth Longfellow, Emily Dickinson, and Walt Whitman.

1865–1900: Realistic Period

The United States entered this period following the Civil War. The major genre of the literature of this time is realistic fiction. This type of literature uses believable characters in scenarios that might actually happen. The focus of these works is on the commonplace and the ordinary. Major writers of the period include Mark Twain, Henry James, Bret Hart, and Kate Chopin.

1900–1914: Naturalistic Period

During this period, writers attempted to represent people and events with even more accuracy than had the writers of the Realistic Period. These writers produced characters who are merely higher-order animals whose behavior is entirely based on heredity and environment. The authors of this period presented their subjects with scientific objectivity. Notable writers of the time were Stephen Crane, Jack London, and Theodore Dreiser.

1914–1939: American Modernist Period

This was similar to the British Modern Period. Writers in this period experimented with subject matter, form, and style and produced in various genres. Some poets of the period are Robert Frost, William Carlos Williams, Edna St. Vincent Millay, and e. e. cummings. Writers of prose during this period include Edith Wharton, Sinclair Lewis, and Willa Cather.

Subclasses of the Modernist Period during the 1920s include the Jazz Age, the Harlem Renaissance, and the Lost Generation. F. Scott Fitzgerald is considered a writer of the Jazz Age, while Langston Hughes and W. E. B. DuBois are considered writers of the Harlem Renaissance. Gertrude Stein, T. S. Eliot, Ezra Pound, and Ernest Hemingway are writers of the Lost Generation.

1939–Present: Contemporary Period

This period began with the end of World War II and continues into the New Millennium. Among the many writers of this period are Eudora Welty, John Updike, Kurt

Vonnegut, Sylvia Plath, Arthur Miller, Tennessee Williams, Ralph Ellison, Gwendolyn Brooks, Zora Neale Hurston, Alice Walker, Toni Morrison, and Maya Angelou.

REPRESENTATIVE WORKS AND MAJOR AUTHORS OF WORLD LITERATURE

The following authors represent those that have not already been mentioned in listing British and American authors. Once again, this is not meant to be an exhaustive list, as that would be impossible. It is suggested that teachers be familiar with as many of these authors as possible.

Edward Abbey	Milan Kundera
Chinua Achebe	Nella Larsen
Richard Adams	Ursula K. Le Guin
Sherman Alexie	Federico García Lorca
Nelson Algren	Thomas Mann
Aristophanes	D'Arcy McNickle
Paul Auster	N. Scott Momaday
Amiri Baraka	Irvin Morris
Donald Barthelme	Alice Munro
Baudelaire	Robert Musil
Samuel Beckett	Vladimir Nabokov
Jorge Luis Borges	Howard Nemerov
Bertolt Brecht	Pablo Neruda
Charles Bukowski	Friedrich Nietzsche
William S. Burroughs	Frank Norris
Albert Camus	Flannery O'Connor
Lewis Carroll	Kole Omotoso
Raymond Carver	Ovid
Louis-Ferdinand Celine	Walker Percy
Miguel de Cervantes	Plato
Paddy Chayefsky	Ezra Pound
Anton Chekhov	Richard Powers
Sandra Cisneros	Marcel Proust
J. M. Coetzee	Alexander Pushkin
Quentin Crisp	Thomas Pynchon
Dante Alighieri	Ishmael Reed

(continued)

Don DeLillo	John Reed
Joan Didion	Carter Revard
Isak Dinesen	Adrienne Rich
Stephen Dixon	Arundhati Roy
John Dos Passos	Salman Rushdie
Fyodor Dostoevsky	David Sedaris
Alexander Dumas	Mary Shelley
Umberto Eco	Sam Sheppard
David Eggers	Leslie Marmon Silko
Louise Erdrich	Upton Sinclair
Lawrence Ferlinghetti	Wallace Stevens
Gustave Flaubert	Ayn Rand
Gabriel García Márquez	Bram Stoker
William Gass	Jonathan Swift
Nikolai Gogol	Luci Tapahonso
Gunter Grass	Hunter S. Thompson
Joseph Heller	Leo Tolstoy
Herman Hesse	Dalton Trumbo
Homer	Edgardo Vega Yunqué
Nick Hornby	Jules Verne
Aldous Huxley	Voltaire
Henrik Ibsen	Kurt Vonnegut
John Irving	David Foster Wallace
Stephen Graham Jones	Nathaniel West
Franz Kafka	William Carlos Williams
John Keats	Sloan Wilson
Jerzy Kosinski	Richard Wright
Ken Kesey	Howard Zinn
Jamaica Kincaid	Emile Zola
Maxine Hong Kingston	

Some major works of world literature include the following:

Bellow, Saul	*The Adventures of Augie March*
Bradbury, Ray	*Fahrenheit 415*
Brontë, Charlotte	*Jane Eyre*
Cather, Willa	*My Antonia*

(continued)

Hardy, Thomas	*Tess of the D'Urbervilles*
Hawthorne, Nathaniel	*The Scarlet Letter*
Orwell, George	*1984*
Plath, Sylvia	*The Bell Jar*
Salinger, J. D.	*Catcher in the Rye*
Steinbeck, John	*The Grapes of Wrath*
Chandler, Raymond	*Farewell, My Lovely*
Conrad, Joseph	*Heart of Darkness*
Eliot, T. S.	*The Waste Land*
Ellison, Ralph	*The Invisible Man*
Lee, Harper	*To Kill a Mockingbird*
Lewis, Sinclair	*Babbitt*
London, Jack	*The Call of the Wild*
Mailer, Norman	*The Naked and the Dead*
Melville, Herman	*Moby Dick*
Miller, Arthur	*Death of a Salesman*
Morrison, Toni	*Beloved*
Wells, H. G.	*The Time Machine*
Wharton, Edith	*The Age of Innocence*
Whitman, Walt	*Leaves of Grass*
Williams, Tennessee	*A Streetcar Named Desire*

APPROPRIATE MATERIALS, TECHNIQUES, AND METHODS FOR TEACHING LITERATURE

How do teachers select appropriate materials for teaching literature to their students? Teachers usually have a general idea of what interests their students and search for specific works that address those interests. Interest inventories are available for teachers to use to narrow student interests and provide targeted guidance on book selection.

In addition, award-winning books can form the basis of literature studies. Every year, the American Library Association confers the Caldecott and Newbery Medals. The Caldecott is awarded to the illustrator of the best picture book for children, and the Newbery is awarded for the most distinguished contribution to children's literature. The winning books and the runners-up are often good choices for literature study. Other awards that can identify outstanding literature for young people are the Coretta Scott King Award,

FTCE Tip

Award-winning books
are often good choices
for your class.

given to one black author and one black illustrator for their inspirational contributions to children's literature, and the Children's Choices, a list of favorite books for different levels of youngsters, arrived at as a result of the votes of ten thousand school children from various regions of the country. In addition, Teachers' Choice is a list of books selected by teachers as excellent for curriculum use and reading aloud.

Several periodicals are available to assist teachers in staying aware of new and outstanding books for youngsters; these include the *Horn Book Magazine, Language Arts, Book Links, Childhood Education, The Reading Teacher,* and the *Journal of Adolescent and Adult Literacy* (Roe and Ross 2006).

There are many approaches to teaching literature. The following is a list of some strategies that have proven particularly effective:

- Have students construct a plot diagram, adding events as they read.

- Have students rewrite the ending of the book.

- Have students rewrite a section of the book from the perspective of a character other than the one from which the story was originally told.

- Have students research the actual events on which a work of historical fiction is based. Compare the book's account with history's account and note discrepancies.

- Have students read a biography or autobiography of the author to determine if and how events in his/her life might have influenced his/her work.

- Construct on the board a web of literary elements—such as title, theme, conflict, setting, and characterization—and have students complete the web.

- Have the students develop a character description of some of the major characters in the book. Pair the students; then have each pair read their character descriptions to one another and correctly identify each other's character.

- Have artistically talented students create a book jacket for a work they have read.

- After reading a book by a contemporary author, have students write a letter to the author, including their response to the book and asking any questions they might have about the inspiration for the book or plot-related questions that they felt were not completely answered by the book.

- Form classroom book clubs. Allow each club to select a book of interest from a list. Schedule regular club meetings during which the students discuss the book.

- Have the students keep double-entry journals. In the left column of the journal, students write direct quotations from the book. In the right column, they write their individual responses, reactions to, or interpretations of the quotation.

- After reading a biography, have the students compare the facts presented with those furnished from informational books. This should be done in chart form so the two sets of data can be easily compared. Based on the findings, the students can determine the degree of authenticity of the biography.

Many other approaches for teaching and sharing literature exist. A teacher's creativity comes into play when deciding how to do this. In addition, many language arts texts include specific suggestions for sharing categories of literature and even specific books with youngsters. These resources can be good sources of inspiration.

REPRESENTATIVE YOUNG ADULT LITERATURE AND ITS CONTRIBUTION TO PERSONAL, SOCIAL, AND ACADEMIC DEVELOPMENT

The genre of realistic fiction is an appropriate place to find books for young adults that will help them in their personal, social, and academic development. A few of the many books that can be used for this purpose are listed here:

- *Little Women*, by Louisa May Alcott (1868), is a classic. Today's students can still relate to this particularly well-written novel. The plot involves a family of four daughters and their mother, waiting for their father to return from the Civil War. Today's families are experiencing similar events while waiting for someone to return from Iraq or Afghanistan. The family love, good neighbors, rich and demanding aunt, and other characters and emotions expressed in this story are as contemporary today as they were when the book was written.

- *Anne of Green Gables,* by L. M. Montgomery (1908), is another classic novel, the first of eight books that describe the life of an orphan living in Canada. The books follow her life from childhood to adulthood. Although the book is set in a period a century distant from today, Anne has many experiences that students will recognize as relevant to them.

- *Sounder,* by William H. Armstrong (1969), has also become a classic. It focuses on the harsh events in the lives of an African-American sharecropper and his family. This Newbery Award–winning book provides great insight into the treatment of African Americans in early times in this country.

- *The Outsiders,* by S. E. Hilton (1967), is a novel depicting life as a gang member. Students today can relate to the relationships among the gang members and gain a better understanding of what compels some young people to become gang members.

- *The Pinballs,* by Betsy Byars (1977), the story of the obstacles overcome by three foster children, is one to which many students can relate.

- *Hatchet,* by Gary Paulsen (1897), is about a 13-year-old boy who successfully lands a plane in the wilderness. The boy's parents are divorced, a situation to which many students can relate.

- *Scorpions,* by Walter Dean Myers (1988), is a novel with believable interracial characters who confront gangs, guns, and murder.

- *A Kind of Thief,* by Vivien Alcock (1992), tells of a 13-year-old girl whose father is arrested for embezzlement and leaves behind a locked briefcase.

Reading biographies and autobiographies, often in the form of journals or diaries, is a useful way to convey a sense of history to students, particularly to students who dislike history. Here are just a few examples of the many books teachers can use for this purpose:

- *Zlata's Diary: A Child's Life in Serajevo* (1995) by Zlata Filipović

- *The Diary of a Young Girl* (1947) by Anne Frank

- *The Way West: Journal of a Pioneer Woman* (1999, based on a journal dated 1853) by Amelia Stewart Knight

The subgenre of informational books can be used to enhance various subjects through literature. Here are some books useful for this purpose:

- *Abraham Lincoln's World,* by Genevieve Foster (1944), is a Newbery winner that depicts the life and times of our sixteenth president.

- *Leonardo da Vinci, by* Diane Stanley (1995), depicts the Renaissance culture of Florence and the life and works of the great artist.

- *Hurricanes: Earth's Mightiest Storms*, by Patricia Lauber (1995), does what its title implies: it thoroughly explains the origins and typical locations of hurricanes. It includes maps, diagrams, and historical and contemporary photos.

Regardless of the topic, there are usually informational books on different reading levels available. A good resource for finding them is *The Book Finder*, which is arranged by subject matter.

APPROPRIATE METHODS FOR ASSESSING THE UNDERSTANDING OF LITERATURE

Students can demonstrate their understanding of literature in numerous ways besides taking traditional paper-and-pencil tests. Among the alternatives teachers can use are literature logs, literature circles, and book conferences. Literature logs are written responses that students provide after reading specific selections. These responses form the basis of group discussions focused on a piece of literature that everyone in the group has read. Book conferences are held between a student and the teacher. These conferences allow the student and teacher, both of whom have read the same book, the opportunity to share ideas they gained from the book, their feelings about the book, and the pleasure the book provided. Most readers have a desire to share their experiences with a book and a book conference gives them the chance to do so. Literature circles are groups that come together for the specific purpose of discussing a designated book, literary genre,

FTCE Tip

Literature logs, literature circles, and book conferences are good alternatives to paper-and-pencil tests.

or author. Sometimes these groups are referred to as grand conversations or literature response groups.

Other means used for assessment include checklists, running records, independent reading inventories, anecdotal records, and rubrics. These have been described and discussed in previous chapters.

REFERENCES

Goforth, F. S. (1998). *Literature and the learner.* Belmont, CA: Wadsworth Publishing Company.

Prentice Hall Literature: World masterpieces. 1996. 4th ed. Upper Saddle River, NJ: Prentice Hall.

Roe, B. D., and E. P. Ross. 2006. *Integrating language arts through literature and thematic units.* Boston: Allyn & Bacon.

Senn, J. A. and Skinner, C. A. 1995. *Heath English: An integrated approach to writing, Teacher's ed.* Lexington, MA: D. C. Heath & Co.

Knowledge of Listening, Viewing, and Speaking as Methods for Acquiring Critical Literacy

EFFECTIVE SPEAKING SKILLS FOR VARIOUS OCCASIONS, AUDIENCES, AND PURPOSES

Students need to develop different speaking skills for different occasions. Types of speaking include persuasive speaking, debate, informative speaking, conversation, panel discussion, oral report, and Reader's Theater.

Persuasive Speaking

A speaker uses persuasive speaking to convince an audience of a particular point of view or position on an issue. Students need to learn about the three methods they can use to persuade. First, persuasion can be based on reason and can use facts. Second, persuasion can be based on an appeal to character. If the listener trusts someone, the speaker can persuade by virtue of the recommendation of the trusted person. Third, persuasion can be based on an appeal to emotions. Some emotions used by persuasive speakers include concern for someone or something, fear, the need for acceptance, and a desire for freedom. Students should have experience in making persuasive speeches using each of the three approaches.

Debate

"Debates are formal discussions of a topic, question, or issue with opposing sides of an argument presented." Divide youngsters into pairs or small groups. Normally, one member or half of the small group takes the pro side, or supports the issue, while the other side takes the con position, or argues against the issue. "In formal debates, there is a moderator who introduces and concludes the debate. The audience judges and decides on the winning team" (Bromley 1998, 329). One side begins the debate with a statement in favor of the proposition. The other side counters with a statement against the proposition. The two sides alternate as they present the two sides with statements and rebuttals. In judging the winning side of the debate, the teacher should consider the following questions: How clearly did the speakers communicate their ideas to the audience? Did the speakers' arguments show thorough knowledge of the topic? Were the two sides courteous to each other? Did the team members cooperate with one another? Did the speakers use and extend the arguments of the teammates who preceded them? To assess the performance of members of debating teams, a teacher can use a rubric similar to the one shown here.

Informative Speaking

Informative speaking allows students to share information they have with an audience. Students need to research their topics thoroughly to make certain that they are knowledgeable and comfortable in making their presentations. The teacher should encourage students to use visual aids such as charts, graphs, PowerPoint slides, diagrams, or photographs.

Conversation

Conversations in class also encourage students to share information and opinions. "The most effective discussions are those in which there is a real opportunity to do more than repeat ideas from the book, film, or lecture. Discussions should do more than give

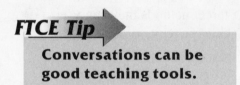

FTCE Tip

Conversations can be good teaching tools.

the predetermined correct answers; they should give students the opportunity to analyze or speculate and to present their own ideas" (Fisher and Terry 1990, 484). Class discussions can take many forms. The following are a few examples of topics for class discussions: "analyze propaganda in commercials and advertisements, compare characters in a book and video versions of a story, brainstorm questions for an interview, design a mural or bulletin board display, assess the effectiveness of a cross-age tutoring program, [and] share writing

Debate Rubric

Resolved: There should be more sports for students at South Rock Creek School.

Rating Code: 1–5, 5 = highest, 1 = lowest

	Appearance	Delivery	Factual information	Keeping to the point	Persuasiveness	Teamwork	Participation in rebuttal	Total
Pro								
Sundee Aday	____	____	____	____	____	____	____	____
James Zientek	____	____	____	____	____	____	____	____
Jeremy Bailey	____	____	____	____	____	____	____	____
							Total	____
Con								
Melody Brooks	____	____	____	____	____	____	____	____
Whitney Lawson	____	____	____	____	____	____	____	____
Darth Taylor	____	____	____	____	____	____	____	____
							Total	____

Source: Tompkins (1998, 301).

in writing groups and get feedback from classmates about how to revise rough drafts"
(Tompkins 1998, 307). From engaging in class conversations and discussions, students
can learn appropriate ways to begin a conversation, take turns, keep a discussion moving
forward, support what others have to say, deal appropriately with conflict, and bring the
discussion to a close.

Panel Discussion

A special type of discussion that students need to experience is a panel discussion. A
panel discussion, sometimes called a roundtable discussion, allows a panel of students to

become experts on specific aspects of a topic and to make a presentation in a comfortable group format. The panel is seated in front of the class, and each member of the panel presents the subtopic he or she researched. Then all panel members discuss the topic together, sharing their information, and invite audience members to ask questions. A panel may have a moderator responsible for ensuring that all students have an equal opportunity to participate and bringing the discussion to its conclusion.

Oral Report

Oral reports also give students an opportunity to present information to the class on a topic that they have researched. Students are taught to ask themselves the following questions when preparing to give an oral report: "What is my purpose? Who is the audience? How long should it be? Do content and form of delivery fit the audience?" (Bromley 1998, 330).

Reader's Theater

Readers' Theater can be an entertaining way for students to gain confidence in front of an audience and improve their reading fluency. While reading (not reciting) extracts from literature, students should attempt to bring the story to life for the listeners.

> In Readers' Theater a story, a section of a book or a poem is brought to life by the 'readers,' who prepare the reading so that they can use their voices to create the characters and events. Typically, there are no costumes or props, and the readers sit on tall stools with their scripts in hand during the presentations. Preparations for such a dramatization may include extensive discussion and analysis of the literature. (Fisher and Terry 1990, 289)

Students prepare their own scripts for Readers' Theater and thus combine literature reading, writing, speaking, and listening.

EFFECTIVE STRATEGIES AND TECHNIQUES FOR LISTENING

Just as there are many types of writing, there are many types of listening. These include marginal, appreciative, attentive, and analytical. *Marginal listening* means that the listener is aware of sound in the immediate environment but is not actively responding to it. *Appreciative listening* means that the listener is responding to poetry, music, or literature in terms of creative and expressive thoughts; enjoyment is key to appreciative listening. *Attentive listening* requires the listener to focus on what is heard to gain information. Sometimes attentive listening involves following directions, identifying the main idea, following a sequence of activities, or participating in a class discussion. *Analytical listening* requires listeners to interpret or evaluate what they heard and judge the accuracy of the information.

Factors that affect listening are hearing, listening, and auding. Hearing relates to the physical aspects of listening. Hearing involves auditory acuity and binaural considerations. Auditory acuity involves the ability to hear sounds over a range of tones and at different levels of volume. Binaural considerations relate to the ability to hear adequately from both ears simultaneously. Listening refers to taking in sounds, analyzing, recognizing, and associating them with meaning. Finally, auding means taking meaning from what is heard and then making comparisons, cataloging ideas, noting the sequence of ideas, forming sensory impressions, and appreciating it.

The teacher should provide opportunities for students to engage in each type of listening. In addition, students should set a purpose for listening because it is a critical step in comprehension.

Students should have the necessary background to fully appreciate and understand what they will hear. Discussing a topic before presenting aural information helps students relate to the topic and extract the maximum amount of meaning from what they will hear. It is also helpful if the teacher makes sure that students are aware of the characteristics and typical format of the genre they are about to hear so they know what to expect. Another way to increase the likelihood that students will understand what they hear is to review the vocabulary usually associated with the topic.

Effective strategies to improve students' listening ability include the following:

- Finding key words: As they listen, students write down the key words that will enable them to comprehend what they hear.

- Listen to predict: Students listen to most of a story or book and then predict how it will end. If the students have not engaged in attentive or analytical listening, their predictions will not be accurate.

- Paraphrasing what they heard: After listening to a presentation, chapter, or passage, students paraphrase what they heard, aiming to be as accurate and comprehensive as possible.

- Summarizing aural information: A student presents an oral summary of a speech, television program, or book. The students in the audience judge the accuracy of the summary so that they too have to listen to the original presentation as well as to the summary.

APPROPRIATE METHODS AND STRATEGIES TO ANALYZE PERSUASIVE TECHNIQUES USED TO CONVEY MESSAGES IN MASS MEDIA

Students are bombarded with propaganda techniques in all forms of mass media. Teachers need to help them to become critical listeners who can accurately evaluate what they hear. In particular, students need to become critical consumers of advertising; advertisers most often use deceptive language and propaganda devices.

Doublespeak is a type of deceptive language that is "evasive, euphemistic, confusing, and self-contradictory" and "pretends to communicate but really does not" (Tompkins 1998, 289). A euphemism is used to distort reality and consists of a word or phrase designed to protect someone's feelings, to make the ordinary seem extraordinary, or to deceive. Examples of euphemisms include *civil disorder* (for *riot*), *correctional facility* (for *jail*), *encore telecast* (for *rerun*), *genuine imitation leather* (for *vinyl*), *memorial park* (for *cemetery*), *passed away* (for *died*), *preowned* (for *used*), and *senior citizen* (for *old person*).

Students need to learn to recognize specific propaganda devices so they can respond to them appropriately. Here are some of the most common devices:

- Glittering generalities use terms like *motherhood* or *justice* to enhance the quality of a product or the nature of a political candidate. The terms used are considered universally appealing so that listeners do not think to challenge what the speaker is really saying.

- Testimonials are endorsements offered by well-known personalities. The listener is expected to associate the product with the celebrity and not to question the expertise of the person to judge the quality of the product.

- Transfer relies on the prestige of a spokesperson to convince potential buyers that using the product will make them look as young as the spokesperson, play a sport as well, be as popular, or the like.

- Name-calling involves the use of derogatory references to a competitor's product so that the listener will associate that product with something negative (true or not) and buy the advertised product instead.

- Bandwagon is an approach that focuses on people's desire to be part of a group. A slogan such as "Choosy moms choose ____" is an example of this approach. The advertiser is counting on the consumer to want to be counted among discriminating mothers.

- Snob appeal relies on peoples' desire to belong to an exclusive group. Typically, this device is used to advertise cosmetics, expensive clothing, and gourmet foods. The long-running advertising campaign for a well-known hair coloring is an example of this, as it uses the tagline "I'm worth it."

- Rewards are used by some propagandists to entice consumers to buy their products. For example, children's meals at fast-food restaurants come with toys, and manufacturers offer cash rebates to buyers.

Because students are constantly being wooed by these techniques, it is vital that teachers prepare them to weigh carefully what they are being told so that they can become critical, careful, informed consumers.

ANALYZE MEDIA MESSAGES TO INTERPRET MEANING, METHOD, AND INTENT

The best way to teach about mass media is to build lessons around taped television or radio advertisements or copies of print advertising. For example, the teacher could have students view or listen to an advertisement, determine which propaganda device it employs, and then raise appropriate questions like the following: What does this celebrity know about the product that could convince me to buy it based on this testimonial? Is the generality used in this ad true, or true for me? Is there evidence of bias in the ad? Does the advertiser use deceptive language? Does the advertiser use sweeping generalities or unsupported inferences? Questioning the use of propaganda devices will help students learn not to take everything at face value or to believe everything they read or hear.

After students have analyzed television, radio, and print advertising, they should have the opportunity to create their own commercials incorporating the techniques they have learned. Groups can take turns presenting their ads while classmates analyze them and identify the devices employed.

EVALUATE THE ELEMENTS, USES, AND EFFECTS OF MEDIA

All forms of media combine auditory and visual elements to convey messages, so students should gain experience evaluating both elements. They need to be aware that media often use sounds and images to evoke emotions and that they should not let those emotions get in the way of a rational evaluation of the message. Teachers need to provide students with practice in analyzing various examples of media for the intentional use of sound and imagery to elicit an emotional response. It is a skill that students will need throughout their lives. According to the College Board (2006, 171):

> To be successful in college and in the workplace and to participate effectively in a global society, students are expected to understand the nature of media; to interpret, analyze, and evaluate the media messages they encounter daily; and to create media that expresses a point of view and influences others. These skills are relevant to all subject areas.

Media can be entertaining, persuading, or informing. Students should have the opportunity to analyze media designed to perform each of these functions. They can work together to create a checklist for evaluating each type of media and then use the checklist to rate various examples.

Activities that students can do to become informed viewers include the following: watch a film adaptation of a book they have read and compare the two versions of the story; critique television shows and report on their educational value; keep a television viewing log of the shows and ads they watch, analyze their viewing habits, and voice ideas about why advertisers support certain shows; focus on violence on television and research the relationship between media-presented violence and what happens in real life; watch the evening news in groups (each group watching a different network) and compare and contrast the presentations; and compare the coverage of the same event in several newspapers.

VARIOUS METHODS FOR ASSESSING LISTENING, VIEWING, AND SPEAKING

Listening

Assessment of listening should occur in various settings and without students' knowledge that they are being evaluated. To assess attentive listening abilities, the teacher can give students oral directions and determine how well they follow them. Oral comprehension is usually determined by reading passages to students and having them answer comprehension questions. The questions usually require students to identify the main idea of the passage, relate facts presented, define vocabulary used, determine cause and effect, draw inferences, and reach conclusions. After using several passages in this way, patterns begin to emerge that enable the teacher to diagnose the types of questions that are causing the greatest number of comprehension problems.

Viewing

Assessment of viewing can involve a written or spoken response to what was viewed. As with oral readings, the teacher can ask questions related to the main idea of the visual, the facts presented and vocabulary used, cause-and-effect relationships presented (if appropriate), and inferences and conclusions.

Speaking

Assessment of speaking "should be performance based and conducted in authentic contexts; it should not be limited to paper and pencil" tests or checklists (Cox 2002, 169). The teacher can use a checklist to evaluate each student's ability to make eye contact, focus on the subject, speak clearly (use proper enunciation and diction), organize ideas, speak with appropriate volume, use visuals to maintain audience interest, make key points, and respond to audience reactions. Oral presentations can also be videotaped to allow students to evaluate their own performances. Each student can use a checklist when viewing the tape and discuss the evaluation with peers and the teacher.

APPROPRIATE TECHNOLOGICAL RESOURCES FOR INSTRUCTIONAL PURPOSES

Word Processing

Teachers can use many technological resources for instructional purposes. The most basic of these is word processing. Allowing students to use word-processing programs on computers might take some of the drudgery out of the writing process and make it easier for students to correct and publish their writing.

E-mail

Electronic messaging or e-mail can enable students to communicate with each other and with others around the world, including the authors of books they have read. Younger students can use e-mail to communicate with older students who can serve as mentors. Teachers can contact peers in other countries and establish e-mail pen pals for their classes. Students can practice language, share cultures, and practice writing skills when contacting these electronic friends.

Internet

The Internet is a worldwide network of information readily available to students. Through the Internet, students can access libraries, museums, schools, and other institutions around the world. Students can learn to use the Internet for research by using a subject directory like Yahoo! or a search engine like Alta Vista to search for sources containing key words.

When using the Internet with students, the teacher should introduce the topic, define it, and determine its importance. Next, the teacher needs to identify tasks related to the topic, such as what questions students need to answer, what problems they need to solve, or what actions they need to take. Relevant Web sites should be listed so that students can find the information they need with relative ease and in a relatively short amount of time. The students should decide on the best way to answer the questions, solve the problems, or take the actions needed.

Hypermedia

The teacher might also wish to introduce students to hypermedia by having them use software such as HyperStudio to complete projects. Hypermedia software enables students to create presentations with various backgrounds, fonts, music, animations, and voice-over narrations. With the software, even novices can produce professional-looking presentations.

Teachers must take necessary precautions when using technology in the classroom. Technology should not become an end in itself. Teachers should try to ensure that all members of a group have an opportunity to engage directly with the technology. If only one student has direct contact with the technology, the other members of the group will stand on the periphery and engage in incidental rather than direct learning. It is possible for computers to become a distraction in the classroom and to interfere with students engaged in other learning activities such as reading. Computer technology is expensive and changes very quickly. It needs to be upgraded frequently and can use up the better part of a school's resources, leaving little for other resources.

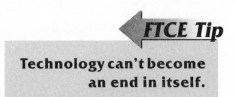

FTCE Tip

Technology can't become an end in itself.

REFERENCES

Bromley, K. D. 1998. *Language arts: Exploring connections*. Upper Saddle River, NJ: Prentice Hall.

College Board. 2006. College Board standards for college success: English language arts. *www.collegeboard.com/prod_downloads/about/association/academic/english-language-arts_cbscs.pdf* (accessed March 20, 2008).

Cox, C. 2002. *Teaching language arts*. Boston: Allyn & Bacon.

Fisher, C. J., and C. A. Terry. 1990. *Children's language and the language arts: A literature-based approach*. Boston: Allyn & Bacon.

Tompkins, G. E. 1998. *Language arts: Content and teaching strategies*. 4th ed. Upper Saddle River, NJ: Prentice Hall.

Knowledge of the Methods for Integration of the Language Arts

METHODS OF INTEGRATING LANGUAGE ARTS

The language arts comprise several elements, and although each has its own unique characteristics, all are connected in a web of interrelated skills. Thus, when students learn one language skill, they typically make advances in others. For example, students who have learned to identify the main idea from an essay or novel will likely be able to discern the main idea of a politician's speech they hear on television because "the cognitive activity is essentially the same after the decoding of oral, written, or visual symbols has taken place" (Roe and Ross 2006).

> Students learn more and at a deeper level when subjects are integrated. The main reason for this is that using language—written or oral—helps students go beyond the facts to the ideas and feelings that control facts. There is a purpose for finding out information and a way to use what they have learned. (Fisher and Terry 1990, 479)

All six of the interrelated language arts—speaking, writing, visually representing, reading, listening, and viewing—are necessary for effective communication, and all involve the skills of thinking and constructing meaning (Roe and Ross 2006). Speaking, writing, and visually representing are expressive language arts. Reading, listening, and viewing are receptive language arts.

Speaking involves constructing a message for the listener with oral symbols (spoken words). Writing involves constructing a message for the reader with written symbols (printed words). Visually representing involves constructing a message for the viewer with visual symbols (pictures, diagrams, maps, graphs, videos, and so on). . . . Listening involves attempting to reconstruct the meaning behind the words of a speaker. . . . Reading involves attempting to reconstruct the meaning behind the words of a writer. . . . Viewing involves attempting to construct the meaning behind visual images that are presented. (Roe and Ross 2006, 17–18)

Integrating Skills

The language arts of listening, speaking, reading, and writing all require knowledge of vocabulary and grammar. The language arts of reading and writing are complementary skills. A person has no reason to write if no one intends to read, and no one can read if nothing has been written.

Use of Literature

One way teachers can integrate the language arts is by using literature. Students can listen to selections from literature read aloud, view presentations and live performances, and read literature themselves. After hearing, viewing, or reading literature, they can write about the selections and visually present information they have gained from them.

Webbing

Another strategy to use when integrating the language arts is webbing. "A web is a visual network of ideas linked to a central theme or focus" (Galda, Cullinan, and Strickland 1993, 315). Constructing a web is a cooperative activity involving students and the teacher. The center of the web can be a theme, a literary genre, a topic, an author, or a specific book. Extending from the center are many arms representing ideas or activities that relate to the center. Because the web can contain many ideas and activities, it should be thought of as a "web of possibilities." Together students and the teacher select ideas and activities for the web that are appropriate to their abilities and interests.

Journals and Learning Logs

Teachers can also integrate language arts using journals and learning logs. As discussed in Chapter 5, many teachers have students keep journals in connection with literature. However, journals or learning logs can be used in any subject area and allow students to write down their reactions, responses, opinions, and general thoughts on any subject they may be studying. Students should share their journals with peers so they can benefit from the perspectives of others. Because journals are not graded, they are not a burden to teachers, and students feel free to express themselves.

Trade Books

Integrating the curriculum across subject areas can be done by using appropriate trade books. These are often of greater interest to students than conventional textbooks and may be written at a level that students can more easily comprehend. Biographies are especially useful in science and social studies.

Math

Incorporating writing into the study of math has also proven useful. Often students "learn" how to solve math problems but do not have a clear understanding of the steps involved. Having students write explanations of their solutions helps them to clarify their understanding and incorporates writing into mathematics. Many trade books are appropriate to the study of math. BookFinder.com is a search engine that is a valuable resource for finding books appropriate to every subject and ability level.

Thematic Teaching

Another way to integrate language arts is to use thematic teaching. "Thematic units can be centered around a topic or theme, a genre of literature, an author, or even a single book. Cross-curricular thematic units combine study in all related content areas that are appropriate to the chosen theme" (Roe and Ross 2006, 23).

ELEMENTS OF COOPERATIVE LEARNING, INCLUDING GROUPING STRATEGIES, GROUP INTERACTIONS, AND COLLABORATION

"Cooperative learning is an instructional technique that uses students' own conversation as a vehicle for learning" (Cox 2002, 162). Research on cooperative learning has found that it increases student achievement and has positive effects on intergroup relations. Some of the positive effects of cooperative learning are increased motivation for learning, increased sharing of metacognitive strategies for thinking and learning, more effective communication skills, and improved social skills (Bromley 1998).

Cooperative Learning

In cooperative learning, the teacher serves as organizer and facilitator rather than as a "walking encyclopedia" who dispenses knowledge. Cooperative learning groups consist of two to six students who work together with a specific purpose, "either to accomplish some sort of task or to discuss a topic for a reason" (Bromley 1998, 322). Many of these groups have a designated leader and a designated scribe. The leader keeps the group on task and helps the group to summarize its work. The scribe takes notes and records the information the group unearths.

Jigsaw

The most well-known and popular cooperative learning structure is called jigsaw. Using this structure, "a task is divided into as many parts as there are groups, and each small group works on a separate part of the problem" (Bromley 1998, 322). At first, each member of the team becomes an "expert" on one topic by working with members of the other teams who are assigned the same subtopic. Students then return to their original groups and share what they have learned about each of their respective subtopics. Everyone on every team is evaluated on the entire topic, including all the subtopics.

Think-Pair-Share

Another cooperative learning strategy is called think-pair-share. "In this type of cooperative learning strategy, students think about a question or topic, pair up with partners to discuss it, and share their thoughts with the rest of the class" (Cox 2002, 163).

Numbered Heads Together

In the cooperative learning strategy called numbered heads together, each member of a small group takes a number and finds the answer to that numbered question on a list of questions furnished by the teacher. When the teacher calls a number, all of the students with that number give their group's answer. Everyone is responsible for learning all the material because the teacher calls the numbers at random.

Roundtable

In the roundtable strategy, a small group of students sits in a circle with one piece of paper and one writing implement. The group members collaborate to answer a question or solve a problem that has several answers. Each student gives an answer orally and writes it on the paper. The paper is passed around the table so everyone can add a response.

These are the most popular forms of cooperative learning. There are several other versions of these and additional strategies as well. Knowledge of those mentioned will serve most language arts teachers well.

APPROPRIATE INTERDISCIPLINARY ACTIVITIES

Many topics are appropriate for interdisciplinary activities incorporating language arts and other content areas. Two units of study and examples of interdisciplinary activities to accompany them are discussed here.

In a unit on energy, students might conduct a survey on opportunities to conserve energy at home and at school; interview energy company officials and write reports on the information they gather; use textbooks, reference materials, the Internet, and other media to collect information and compile it into reports; participate in debates, panel discussions, or roundtable discussions; conduct experiments on energy conservation; make charts, graphs, and diagrams to record information; build models related to energy consumption and conservation; and write to government officials about energy concerns (Roe and Ross 2006).

A unit on pioneer life might include the following activities: using a jigsaw approach, students investigate topics such as travel conditions, home life for pioneer children, and education in pioneer days; using maps of the United States, students mark the routes of pioneers, note the specific hazards on certain routes (mountains, rivers, etc.), and compute the mileage from start to finish; assuming the identity of pioneers, students write a fictional journal telling of their travels; with the help of local artisans recruited by the teacher to visit the class, students make candles or soap, a quilt, or corn husk dolls; students make a timeline showing when various regions of the country were settled; focusing on common problems encountered by pioneers (such as a broken wagon

FTCE Tip

Interesting ideas make for interesting language arts lessons.

wheel, preserving food), students brainstorm solutions; students plan and prepare a menu of typical pioneer foods (corn pone, molasses, dried apples, etc.); students engage in a debate over conflicts between Native Americans and pioneers over territorial rights (Roe and Ross 2006).

ELEMENTS OF AN INTEGRATED LESSON

An integrated lesson incorporates as many content areas as appropriate to the topic and the students. An integrated lesson includes a behavioral objective, a list of materials needed by the students to participate in the lesson and by the teacher to teach the lesson, procedures, questions the teacher plans to ask, assessment activities, and plans to follow up the lesson.

Unlike a more traditional lesson, an integrated lesson includes objectives, procedures, and activities that span several content areas instead of just one. As a result, assessment of an integrated lesson is somewhat more involved than in a traditional lesson because it necessitates the evaluation of learning in several diverse content areas, rather than in only one.

Integrating instruction is an approach that should be adopted in all areas of the curriculum but especially in language arts instruction. The language arts encompass more subtopics and areas of instruction than any other subject. Integrating instruction across curriculum areas makes instruction and learning more relevant and interesting, and it gives the teacher more time to include the wide variety of skills and concepts the subject includes. Without integration, teachers would surely run out of the time needed to teach long before they run out of the knowledge and skills they need to teach.

REFERENCES

Bromley, K. D. 1998. *Language arts: Exploring connections.* Upper Saddle River, NJ: Prentice Hall.

Cox, C. 2002. *Teaching language arts.* Boston: Allyn & Bacon.

Fisher, C. J., and C. A. Terry. 1990. *Children's language and the language arts: A literature-based approach.* Boston: Allyn & Bacon.

Galda, L., B. E. Cullinan, and D. S. Strickland. 1993. *Language, literacy and the child.* New York: Harcourt Brace.

Roe, B. D., and E. P. Ross. 2006. *Integrating language arts through literature and thematic units.* Boston: Allyn & Bacon.

Ability to Write Well on a Selection from Poetry or Prose, Including Fiction or Nonfiction

8

The English 6–12 subject area test contains an essay item and lined paper for use in writing your answer. The 60 minutes allotted for this section of the exam includes time to prepare, write, and edit your essay.

The essay section represents 30 percent of the total score of the exam. Two judges will score your work. The personal views you express will not be an issue; however, the skill with which you express those views, the logic of your arguments, and the degree to which you support your position will be very important in the scoring.

The judges will look at not only the substance of your essay but also the composition skills you demonstrate, such as your thesis and focus, organization, style (diction and sentence structure), and mechanics (capitalization, punctuation, spelling, and usage). Your essay will receive points based on specific criteria as follows:

7	The essay has a clear thesis, unity, focus, and a distinctive style. The ideas are concrete, plentiful, appropriate, and deeply textured. The writer uses an abundance of specific, relevant details, including concrete examples that clearly support generalizations.
5	The essay has a thesis, focus, and unity and is clearly written, observing the elements of style. The writer presents a considerable quantity of relevant and specific detail in support of the subject. The sentence patterns vary, and sentence constructions indicate that the writer has facility in the use of language. Effective transitions are accompanied by sentences constructed with orderly relationship between word groups. There may be a few errors in usage, spelling, capitalization, and punctuation.
3	The essay has some degree of unity and focus, but it is only reasonably clear. The writer employs a limited number of specific details relating to the subject. Paragraphs are usually sufficiently unified and developed. Sentence variety is minimal. Some transitions are used, and parts are related to each other in an orderly manner. The essay is awkward at times. Usage is generally accurate. Some errors in spelling, capitalization, and punctuation exist, detracting from the essay's effect and its sense.
1	The essay lacks unity and focus. The writer includes very little, if any, specific and relevant supporting detail but instead uses unsupported generalizations. Paragraphs are underdeveloped and ineffective. Sentences lack variety. Transitions and coherence are not discernible. The essay contains many errors in usage, spelling, capitalization, and punctuation. An off-topic essay will automatically be classified in category 1.

Carefully read the assignment before you begin to write. Think about your ideas and what you would like to communicate to the reader. To help organize your thoughts, you might want to make an outline of your essay on scratch paper, but be sure to write the final draft of your response in the test booklet. Your score will be based on what you write in that booklet. When you have finished writing, be sure to review your work and make any changes you believe would enhance your score.

This review will guide you through a systematic process of how to write an essay, from writing strategies to budgeting time during the exam. Even if you feel that you are a good writer, you should study the review because it will help you become familiar with essay writing. The strategies presented here will help you write an essay that is to the point, easily understood, properly structured, well supported, and correct according to the rules of grammar. You need not write a best-selling book to pass this test. Remember, the more you practice the strategies provided in this review, the easier it will be for you to write a good essay.

STRATEGIES FOR THE ESSAY

The following study plan will maximize your chances of receiving a passing score on your essay:

Step 1   Study this review to enhance your ability to write an essay. Remember, the sharper your skills, the more likely you are to receive a passing score on your writing sample.

Step 2   Practice writing an essay. The best way to do this is to complete the practice tests included in this book.

Step 3   Learn and understand the directions, so you do not waste valuable time reading them on the test day. This will allow you to review them quickly before writing your essay.

Step 4   Develop your essay from the notes you have made. Present your position clearly and logically, making sure to provide adequate examples and/or support. Write your draft on scratch paper.

Step 5   Proofread your essay! Check every word for errors in spelling. Be sure that your sentences are concise and grammatically correct. Make any necessary revisions.

Step 6   Copy the final version of your essay into the response booklet.

Here are some additional tips for writing a good essay:

* Be sure that you have not strayed from your topic or introduced points that you have not explained.

* Vary the types of sentences you include so that your essay flows smoothly and is easy to read.

* Use vocabulary that suits your audience. You do not want to insult your audience by using simple vocabulary or by explaining things they already know. Likewise, do not alienate your audience by using complicated jargon or by assuming that they are already familiar with the subject on which you are writing.

EFFECTIVE ESSAY WRITING

Some of the best thinkers have written essays that we continue to read from generation to generation. An essay offers the reader a logical, coherent, and imaginative written composition showing the nature or consequences of a single controlling idea when considered from the writer's unique perspective. Essays always express more or less directly the author's opinion, belief, position, or knowledge (backed by evidence) about the idea or object in question. For the FTCE test, you will need to recognize and generate the elements of an excellent essay. In essence, you will be taking the principles covered in this review and using them to create your own original essay.

Academic essay writing has two primary purposes: (1) persuasion through argumentation and (2) informing and educating through analysis. When an essay consists of an argument, the writer uses organizational strategies to present reasons and evidence to persuade readers to see an issue the writer's way. An informative essay presents information on a specific topic for the enlightenment of the readers. Regardless of the essays purpose, the issue or topic the writer presents is the essay's thesis, and the writer uses the appropriate organizational strategies to demonstrate the thesis.

The following are seven methods you can use to prove a thesis:

1. Show how a process or procedure does or should work, systematically, in time.

2. Compare or contrast two or more things or ideas to show important differences or similarities.

3. Identify a problem and then explain how to solve it.

4. Analyze an idea or topic into components or classify it by type or category to show how it is put together, how it works, or how it is designed.

5. Explain why something happens to produce a particular result or set of results.

6. Describe a particular characteristic or feature of a place, person(s), time, or idea.

7. Define what a thing is or what an idea means.

Depending on the purpose of the essay, one pattern tends to dominate the discussion question. For example, the writer might use description and explanation to define the varied meanings of *love*.

During the FTCE test, you will need to exercise control over your writing by following the writing process and knowing the pitfalls of weak writing and correcting them. Using the steps outlined in this review will help you do that. Make any corrections you need during the appropriate stage of the writing process; to correct errors at the wrong stage could waste time and interfere with your effort to produce the best essay response.

COMPOSING YOUR ESSAY: USING THE WRITING PROCESS

Some people think that writers can just sit down and churn out wonderful essays or poems in one sitting, in a flash of genius and inspiration. That is not true. Writers use the writing process from start to finish to help ensure that their work is clear and meaningful. If you do not reflect on your composition in stages and make changes as you develop it, you will not see all the problems or errors in it. You cannot expect that the first version of the essay you write will be the final version. Before you turn in your test essay and leave the room, you will need to read through it, reflect, and revise, using the entire writing process.

The writing process has five steps:

1. prewriting, or planning time

2. rough draft

3. organizing and revising the main ideas (not the words or sentences themselves at this point)

4. polishing, or editing (making sure sentences are complete, that the words you use are the right words, and that the spelling and punctuation are correct)

5. proofreading, to make sure all mistakes are corrected

Using this process does not mean that you have to write five drafts. Write one draft (steps 1 and 2), leaving space for corrections (e.g., write on every other line), and then work on the draft through the rest of the steps (3 through 5). If time allows, you might want to do the whole process on scrap paper and then copy the finished product onto the allotted test paper. If you do choose to work on scrap paper and then copy it, make sure you proofread your copy to see whether, while transcribing it, you left anything out, or wrote a word twice or made any other errors.

Prewriting

Establishing Your Thesis

Read the essay question and decide on your thesis. For example, suppose the test question is, "Do you agree or disagree with the statement 'Television is a bad influence on people.'?"

Your first step is to decide whether you agree or disagree. Take a definite stand; do not be noncommittal. If you feel very strongly, take that position because it will be the easiest for you to write about. If you do not feel strongly either way, take the side you think you might have the most to write about. The position you take is not a factor in the grading of your essay; you are only graded on how well you write.

Whichever position you decide to take, write it down. For example, you might take this position: "I agree that television is a bad influence on people" or "Television is an excellent learning tool and is a good influence on most people." Your position statement is your thesis.

Consider Your Audience

The writer's responsibility is to write clearly and cleanly for the reader's sake. Essays would be pointless without an audience. Why write an essay if no one wants or needs to read it? Why add evidence, organize your ideas, or correct bad grammar? The reason to do any of these things is that someone out there needs to understand what you are writing. What would the audience need to know to understand the points you are making? Visualize someone you know listening to you declare your position or opinion then saying, "Oh yeah? Prove it!"

In writing your essay, make sure to answer the following questions: What evidence do you need to prove your idea to this skeptic? On what points would a skeptic disagree with you? What does the skeptic share with you as common knowledge? What does he or she need to be told by you?

Control Your Point of View

We may write essays from one of three points of view, depending on the essay's audience:

- Subjective or personal point of view: "I think cars are more trouble than they are worth."

- Second person: "If you own a car, you soon find out that it is more trouble than it is worth."

- Third person (focuses on the idea, not what "I" think of it): "Cars are more trouble than they are worth."

Once you decide on a point of view, stick with it. Any of the three is acceptable, but it is important not to switch at any point in your essay.

Support Your Thesis

Your next prewriting step is to jot down a few phrases presenting ideas and examples that support your thesis statement, or your main idea. Do this quickly on a separate piece of paper for about five minutes. Do not try to outline, simply list things that you think might be important to discuss. After you have listed several, pick at least three to five points you want or need to discuss, and number them in the order of importance that is relevant to proving your main idea.

Rough Draft

Providing Evidence

Spend about 10 to 20 minutes writing your rough draft. Looking over your prewriting list, write down what you think is useful to prove your thesis in the order you think will best convince the reader. You can employ any one of the seven steps listed earlier in the chapter to prove your thesis. Be sure to use real evidence from your life experience or knowledge to support what you say. Listed here are the kinds of evidence you can use to support the thesis of your essay:

- Anecdotal evidence: stories from the writer's own experience and knowledge that illustrate a particular point or idea.

- Hard data (facts, statistics, scientific evidence, research): documented evidence that has been verified to be true.

- Expert opinions: assertions or conclusions, usually by authorities, about the matter under discussion.

- Analogies: examples that show a resemblance between one phenomenon and another.

In test situations, most essayists use anecdotal evidence or analogies to prove a thesis. The judges grading your test do not expect you to draw evidence from books; your own life is equally appropriate. For example, if your thesis is "Cars are more trouble to fix than bicycles," you can provide evidence for your idea by citing examples from your own experience: "For example, my father's Buick needs 200 parts to make one brake work, but my bicycle only has four pieces that make up the brakes, and I can replace those myself." Of course, if you know salient facts or statistics, do not hesitate to use them.

Write naturally and quickly. Do not worry too much at this point about paragraphing, spelling, or punctuation—just write down the points you want to make in the order you indicated on your list.

Transitions

To help readers follow the flow of your ideas and to help unify the essay, use transitions to show the connections between ideas. You can use transitions either at the beginnings of paragraphs to connect larger ideas or at the beginning of sentences to show how the more specific points in a single paragraph are connected.

Here are some typical transitional words and phrases that you should use when writing your essay.

To link similar ideas, use the following words:

again	equally important	in addition	or
also	for example	in like manner	similarly
and	for instance	likewise	too
another	further	moreover	
besides	furthermore	of course	

To link dissimilar or contradictory ideas, use words like the following:

although	conversely	instead	otherwise
and yet	even if	nevertheless	provided that
as if	however	on the contrary	still
but	in spite of	on the other hand	yet

To indicate cause, purpose, or result, use these words:

as a result	for	since	therefore
as consequently	for this reason	so	thus
because	hence	then	

To indicate time or position, use words like these:

above	at the present time	first	second
across	before	here	thereafter
afterward	beyond	meanwhile	thereupon
around	eventually	next	
at once	finally	presently	

To indicate an example or summary, use phrases such as the following:

as a result	in any case	in conclusion	in short
as I have said	in any event	in fact	on the whole
for example	in brief	in other words	to sum up
for instance			

Organizing and Reviewing Paragraphs

The unit of work for revising is the paragraph. After you have written what you wanted to say based on your prewriting list, spend about 20 minutes revising your draft by looking to see whether you need to indent for paragraphs anywhere. If you do, make a proofreader's mark (¶) to indicate to the reader that you think a paragraph should start there. Check whether you need to add anything that would make your thesis more convincing. If you do not have room on the paper to add the new paragraph in the appropriate spot, add that paragraph at the end of your essay and indicate with a number or some other mark where it should be. Ensure that you gave examples or illustrations for your statements and used transitions to connect your ideas.

Following are two sample paragraphs: one without concrete evidence for its idea and one with evidence. Study each. Note the topic sentence and how that sentence is or is not supported with evidence.

> Television is a bad influence on people. Programs on television are often stupid and depict crimes that people later copy. Television takes time away from loved ones, and it often becomes addictive. Therefore, television is bad for people because it is no good.

In this example, the writer has not given any concrete evidence for the ideas presented. The writer just declares them to be so. Any of the sentences in the paragraph might make a good opening sentence for a whole paragraph. Take the second sentence, for example:

> Watching television takes time away from other things. For example, all those hours people spend sitting in front of the tube, they could be working on building a chair or fixing the roof. Maybe a man has laundry to do but watches television instead. When Monday comes around and he has no socks to wear to work, he might regret his decision to see that episode of "Everybody Loves Raymond." A woman could have written a letter to a friend whom she has not written to for months, or she could have enjoyed a beautiful day in the park, but because she had to see "General Hospital," she missed the opportunity. Reruns on television are inevitable, but a good friend or a beautiful day is too precious to squander.

> Watching television definitely keeps people from getting things done.

The four pieces of evidence the author uses here are largely anecdotal. *Always* supply evidence. Three is a useful number of examples or illustrations to use in each paragraph. Do not belabor a single point; you do not have time.

For a typical test essay to be fully developed, it should have about five paragraphs. They ought to be organized in the following manner:

- Introduction: A paragraph that shows your main point (thesis) and introduces your position with three general ideas that support your thesis.

- Development: Three middle paragraphs that prove your position from different angles, using evidence from real life and knowledge. Each supporting paragraph in the middle should in turn support each of the three ideas you started out with in the introductory or thesis paragraph.

- Conclusion: The last paragraph, which sums up your position and adds one final reminder of what the issue was, perhaps points to a solution. Here is an example:

    Therefore, by taking away from the quality of life, television is a bad influence on people. We should be watching the sun, the sky, the birds, and each other, not the "boob tube."

Check for Logic

Make sure that you present your argument in a logical manner. If you have not, you may not have proven your point. Your conclusion must follow from a logical set of premises. Watch for the following errors in reasoning when presenting an argument:

- Either/or dilemma: assuming that only two opposing reasons are possible: "You are either with us or against us."

- Oversimplification: reducing the causes of a complicated issue to just one: "The violence that pervades TV shows proves that watching television causes people to become violent.

- Begging the question: basing an argument on a point that is assumed to be true but should be proven to the reader: "The death penalty is an intentional act of killing a person and therefore is murder."

- Ignoring the issue: arguing against the truth of an issue because of its conclusion: "John is a good boy and therefore did not rob the store."

- Arguing against a person, not an idea: arguing that the reason an idea has no merit is that the person presenting the idea is immoral or personally stupid. "Because Eric is failing English, his assertion that the teacher is incompetent cannot be true."

- Non sequitur: leaping to the wrong conclusion: "Jake is from Canada, so he must play hockey."

- Drawing the wrong conclusion from a sequence: attributing the outcome to the wrong reasons: "Betty married an older man at a young age and now has three children, so she is a housewife."

Polishing and Editing Your Essay

If the unit of work for revising is the paragraph, the unit of work for editing is the sentence. To help you check your paper for mistakes, use the following checklist:

Polishing Checklist

- Are all your sentences *really* sentences, or have you written some fragments or run-on sentences?

- Did you use vocabulary correctly?

- Have you used a word that seems colloquial or too informal?

- Did you leave out punctuation anywhere? Did you use commas, periods, and quotation marks correctly?

- Did you capitalize words correctly?

Proofreading

In the last three to five minutes, read your paper word for word, first forward and then backward, reading from the end to the beginning. Doing so can help you find errors that you may have missed by having read forward only.

Practice Test 1

FTCE English 6–12

This test is also on CD-ROM in our special interactive FTCE English TEST*ware*®. It is highly recommended that you first take this exam on computer. You will then have the additional study features and benefits of enforced timed conditions and instantaneous, accurate scoring. See page 7 for guidance on how to get the most out of our FTCE English software.

ANSWER SHEET FOR PRACTICE TEST 1

1 _____	18 _____	35 _____	52 _____	69 _____
2 _____	19 _____	36 _____	53 _____	70 _____
3 _____	20 _____	37 _____	54 _____	71 _____
4 _____	21 _____	38 _____	55 _____	72 _____
5 _____	22 _____	39 _____	56 _____	73 _____
6 _____	23 _____	40 _____	57 _____	74 _____
7 _____	24 _____	41 _____	58 _____	75 _____
8 _____	25 _____	42 _____	59 _____	76 _____
9 _____	26 _____	43 _____	60 _____	77 _____
10 _____	27 _____	44 _____	61 _____	78 _____
11 _____	28 _____	45 _____	62 _____	79 _____
12 _____	29 _____	46 _____	63 _____	80 _____
13 _____	30 _____	47 _____	64 _____	81 _____
14 _____	31 _____	48 _____	65 _____	82 _____
15 _____	32 _____	49 _____	66 _____	83 _____
16 _____	33 _____	50 _____	67 _____	84 _____
17 _____	34 _____	51 _____	68 _____	85 _____

TIME: 1½ hours   85 questions
        1 hour   1 essay question

1. The English language is described as a living language because

    A. it is currently spoken by living people.

    B. it can be used to refer to living organisms.

    C. it is used to discuss life and living things.

    D. it changes due to growth and decay.

2. English has changed over time due to all of the following **EXCEPT**

    A. historical influences.

    B. new science and medical discoveries.

    C. boredom with old vocabulary.

    D. modifications in social attitudes.

3. Romantic poets feel that isolation and alienation are important components to the creation of their poetry. What does alienation have to do with Romantic ideology?

    A. Romantic poets feel isolated and alone.

    B. To commune with nature, one needs to be alone with nature.

    C. Romantic poets feel like aliens in their own country.

    D. Romantic poets feel frustration over foreigners trying to take over their homeland.

4. Hamlin Garlin and Bret Harte used realism to create texts. *Realism* is best defined as

    A. the literary technique of realistically representing the nature of life and the social world, as it would appear to the common reader.

    B. an attempt to subject passive representation to the impressions of natural, monolithic, and flagrant social designs and structures.

  C. the representation of the human condition based on loose and free-flowing designs, patterns, and shapes.

  D. the belief that human beings exist entirely in the order of nature and do not have a soul or any participation in a religious or spiritual world beyond nature.

5. Who is the author attributed with writing *The Iliad* and *The Odyssey?*

  A. Sophocles

  B. Euclid

  C. Homer

  D. Ulysses

6. In the construction of an effective persuasive argument, you must include

  A. a detailed explanation of your personal feelings and emotions as they pertain to the subject matter.

  B. a detailed analysis of the social, literary, and historical contexts upon which the argument is based.

  C. a full recognition and clear analysis of the counterargument showing its strengths and weaknesses.

  D. an oversimplification of the opposing argument, which thereby demonstrates the absurdity of the opposition's point of view.

7. What American author is famous for such works as *Life on the Mississippi* and *Innocents Abroad: or The New Pilgrim's Progress*?

  A. Ambrose Bierce

  B. Stephen Crane

  C. Edgar Allan Poe

  D. Mark Twain

8. What is a topic sentence?

  A. A sentence usually located at the end of a paper that summarizes or concludes the essay

  B. A sentence usually located at the beginning of a paper that follows the rhetorical principles established by Aristotle

C.   A sentence usually located at the beginning of a paper that states the main premise of the essay

D.   A sentence that is usually repeated throughout a paper that reiterates the social or political importance of the essay

9.   What is the definition of *grammar*?

A.   The branch of language study or linguistic study that deals with the means of showing the relationship between words in use

B.   The branch of language study or linguistic study that deals with the specific origins of word roots and their evolution to current and proper usage

C.   The branch of language study or linguistic study that deals with the plant or animal world

D.   The branch of language study or linguistic study that deals with the accuracy of dictionary entries

10.   All of the following are approaches to instruction in grammar **EXCEPT**

A.   literal.

B.   transformational.

C.   traditional.

D.   structural.

11.   The term *alliteration* means which of the following?

A.   A repetitive vowel sound occurring at the beginning of a word or of a stressed syllable within a word

B.   A repetitive consonant sound occurring at the beginning of a word or of a stressed syllable within a word

C.   A repetitive vowel sound occurring at the end of a word or of a stressed syllable within a word

D.   A repetitive consonant sound occurring at the end of a word or of a stressed syllable within a word

Read the following paragraph, then answer questions 12 to 15.

Call me Ishmael. Some years ago—never mind how long precisely—having little or no money in my purse, and nothing particular to interest me on shore. I thought I would sail about a little and see the watery part of the world. It is a way I have of driving off the spleen, and regulating the circulation. Whenever I find myself growing grim about the mouth; whenever it is a damp, drizzly November in my soul; whenever I find myself involuntarily pausing before coffin warehouses, and bringing up the rear of every funeral I meet; and especially whenever my hypos get such an upper hand of me, that it requires a strong moral principle to prevent me from deliberately stepping into the street, and methodically knocking people's hats off—then, I account it high time to get to sea as soon as I can. This is my substitute for pistol and ball. With a philosophical flourish Cato throws himself upon his sword; I quietly take to the ship. There is nothing surprising in this. If they but knew it, almost all men in their degree, some time or other, cherish very nearly the same feelings towards the ocean with me.

Herman Melville, *Moby Dick*, 1851

12. What would you say the overall tone of the paragraph is?

   A.   slow and/or plodding

   B.   angry and/or resentful

   C.   somber and/or melancholy

   D.   jocular and/or optimistic

13. What does the narrator mean when he says, "This is my substitute for pistol and ball"?

   A.   He means that if he does not get to the sea right away, he will kill someone.

   B.   He means that if he must go to sea one more time, he will kill someone.

   C.   He means that if he must go to sea one more time, he will kill himself.

   D.   He means that if he does not get to the sea right away, he will kill himself.

14. The above paragraph is written in what style?

    A. prosaic

    B. poetic

    C. polymorphic

    D. parallel

15. When the narrator refers to "a damp, drizzly November in my soul," he is using what type of figure of speech?

    A. simile

    B. paradigm

    C. trope

    D. metaphor

16. For the purpose of continuity, historians and scholars divide the periods of English literature into various segments. Which of the following puts the segments in the correct chronological order?

    A. Old English, Middle English, Victorian, Renaissance, Romantic, Modern

    B. Old English, Middle English, Renaissance, Romantic, Victorian, Modern

    C. Romantic, Victorian, Middle English, Old English, Modern, Renaissance

    D. Modern, Victorian, Romantic, Renaissance, Middle English, Old English

17. The term that denotes or classifies a recurring type of literature, also called a *literary form*, is more commonly referred to as which of the following?

    A. hyperbole

    B. syntax

    C. zymology

    D. genre

18. Keats, Shelley (Percy Bysshe and Mary), Coleridge, and Wordsworth are names associated with which period of English literature?

    A.   the neoclassical period

    B.   the Victorian period

    C.   the Romantic period

    D.   the Renaissance period

19. Samuel Langhorne Clemens, one of the most famous authors in American history, is known by a more familiar pen name. What is it?

    A.   Ambrose Bierce

    B.   George Eliot

    C.   Mark Twain

    D.   Nathaniel Hawthorne

20. A noun formed from a verb by the addition of –*ing*, as in *run* to *running*, is known as a (an)

    A.   gerund.

    B.   apostrophe.

    C.   anecdote.

    D.   genre.

21. When two independent clauses are **NOT** joined correctly, the sentence is known as a

    A.   fragmented sentence.

    B.   topic sentence.

    C.   run-on sentence.

    D.   comma splice sentence.

22. In the phrase *to boldly go where no man has gone before,* what is the grammatical term for *to boldly go*?

    A.   hyperbolic paradigm

    B.   compound verb

    C.   grammatically correct

    D.   split infinitive

23. Which of the following describes the best practice in writing instruction?

    A. Instruct students in writing, and give them time to write.

    B. Have students complete worksheets about writing.

    C. Have students copy famous speeches.

    D. Have the youngsters create a mural of a story and label all of the characters.

24. Listening is a process students use to extract meaning from oral speech. Activities teachers can engage in to assist students in becoming more effective listeners include:

    I.   clearly setting a purpose for listening.

    II. allowing students to relax by chewing gum during listening.

    III. asking questions about the selection.

    IV. encouraging students to forge links between the new information and knowledge already in place.

    A. I and II

    B. II, III, and IV

    C. I, III, and IV

    D. I, II, III, and IV

25. Read this nursery rhyme, and then choose the letter that contains the words that would occur on the beat.

    > Little boy blue come blow your horn,
    > The sheep's in the meadow, the cow's in the corn,
    > Where is the boy who looks after the sheep?
    > He's under the haystack fast asleep.

    A. Lit, boy, come, your, the, in, dow, cow's, corn. Where, the, who, ter, sheep, under, hay, a.

    B. Lit, blue, blow, horn, sheep's, mea, cow's, corn. Where, boy, aft, sheep, un, hay, fast, sleep.

    C. Lit, blow, sheep's, cow's. Where, aft, under, fast.

    D. Little, The. Where, He's.

26. If a teacher is interested in improving the comprehension skills of students, that teacher should

    I.   teach students to decode well.

    II. allow time during the day to read and reread selections.

    III. discuss the selections after reading to clarify meaning and make connections.

    IV. tell jokes.

    A.   I and II only
    B.   I, II, and IV
    C.   I, II, and III
    D.   I, II, III, and IV

27. *The students in Mrs. Alvarez's class are studying energy conservation. Mrs. Alvarez wants to strengthen her students' ability to work independently. She also wants to provide opportunities for the students to use a variety of print and media resources during this unit of study. Mrs. Alvarez plans to begin the unit by leading the class in a brainstorming session to formulate questions to guide their research about energy conservation.*

    Which of the following criteria should guide Mrs. Alvarez as she leads the brainstorming session?

    A.   The questions should emphasize the factual content presented in the available print materials.

    B.   The questions should emphasize higher-order thinking skills, such as comparison, analysis, and evaluation.

    C.   The questions should reflect the interests of the students.

    D.   The questions should include all of the grade-level objectives for the unit.

28. If a student's purpose is to give an informational speech, he is likely to

    A.   be humorous in his explanation.

    B.   be somewhat repetitive to reinforce points made.

    C.   be sure to incorporate his opinion of the information he is presenting.

    D.   give many reasons for learning the information.

29.   A scoring rubric is designed to

    A.   focus on each aspect of an assigned task.

    B.   allow a teacher to note just the presence or absence of each component of an assignment.

    C.   allow teachers to afford some aspects of an assignment more importance by weighting them more highly.

    D.   both A and C

30.   The primary purpose of an IRI (Informal Reading Inventory) is to

    A.   compute a youngster's instructional reading level.

    B.   compute a youngster's independent reading level.

    C.   diagnose reading difficulties and allow the teacher to provide instruction to remediate skill weaknesses.

    D.   diagnose reading difficulties to determine the youngster's frustration level.

31.   A checklist can be used to assess listening and might reasonably include all of the following **EXCEPT**

    A.   the student's ability to follow directions.

    B.   the student's ability to repeat exactly what was heard.

    C.   the student's ability to make pertinent remarks.

    D.   the student's ability to ask relevant questions following a presentation.

32.   If a second language learner is literate in his native language, it will usually take him how long to acquire CALP (Cognitive Academic Language Proficiency) in the second language?

    A.   1–3 years

    B.   3–5 years

    C.   5–7 years

    D.   7–10 years

33. Specific strategies for integrating language and content for second language learners include all of the following **EXCEPT**

    A. using explicit language modeling.

    B. the presentation of realia.

    C. dictating in the second language.

    D. body language.

34. In order to develop proficient writers, teachers must develop

    A. proficient readers.

    B. proficient speakers.

    C. proficient listeners.

    D. proficient viewers.

35. The authoring cycle consists of

    A. brainstorming, drafting, editing, proofreading, final copy.

    B. constructing a graphic organizer, drafting, proofreading, editing, final copy.

    C. drafting, brainstorming, proofreading, editing, final copy.

    D. brainstorming, drafting, editing, publishing, proofreading.

36. A writing portfolio should be organized by

    A. types or categories of writing (autobiography, book reports, etc.).

    B. the date on which each was written (September–June).

    C. highest to lowest grade (A–F).

    D. lowest to highest grade (F–A).

37. An example of figurative language is a(n)

    A. synonym.

    B. antonym.

    C. proverb.

    D. metaphor.

38. The following words are examples of onomatopoeia:

    A. clear, click, chick, cool.

    B. splash, fizz, pluck, pop.

    C. air, always, anyhow, awful.

    D. blog, blame, bloat, blondes.

39. Which of the following is an example of redundancy?

    A. What I am trying to say is that . . . .

    B. The really hot boiling water . . . .

    C. The at-risk student was from a low socioeconomic home.

    D. It was like Daniel in the lion's den.

40. Which of the following is responsible for the major change in the meaning of the word "gay" in contemporary society?

    A. history

    B. societal attitudes

    C. scientific discoveries

    D. medical breakthroughs

41. Which of the following affects a speaker's use of language?

    A. the age of the listeners

    B. the background experiences of the listeners

    C. the speaker's purpose

    D. all of the above

42. Usually it is more effective to write active rather than passive sentences. A passive sentence puts

    A. the noun before its article.

    B. the object before the subject.

    C. the subject before the object.

    D. the noun before the verb.

43. If a sentence's subject is contained in a noun phrase, then a sentence's predicate must contain which of the following?

    A. additional information pertaining to the noun

    B. an antecedent

    C. a verb phrase

    D. an article

44. The rule for applying a preposition or an article to all members of a series is

    A. that you must use either the preposition or article only before the first term or else repeat it before every term.

    B. that you must use the preposition or article any time a noun or verb phrase is used, regardless of its location in the sentence.

    C. variable, depending on the members of a series and their relationship to the preposition or article.

    D. that both articles and prepositions never appear together in a sentence containing a series.

45. While ambiguous writing can be an obstacle for many novice authors, seasoned veterans of the craft, from Shakespeare to Joyce, use ambiguity for pluralistic effects. What does *ambiguous* mean?

    A. using a vague or ambivalent word or expression when a precise word or phrase is called for

    B. using a literary text or reference, without explicit identification of the text or reference

    C. using a word or phrase that states specifically what the author is trying to say

    D. using a literary text or reference that stipulates the continuity of the jargon in a juxtaposing intertextuality

46. Which of the following activities are considered part of the prewriting phase of the writing process?

    A. delimiting the topic, point of view, organizational format, audience for the piece

    B. length of the piece, genre, audience for the piece

C.   choice of theme, point of view, choice of specific vocabulary to be used

D.   delimiting the topic, choice of theme, length of the piece

47.   A teacher wants to facilitate her students' choice of a writing topic. Strategies for assisting them to do this include

      I.   interest inventories

      II.   journals

      III.   prompts

      IV.   freewriting

A.   I and II

B.   II and III

C.   I, II, and IV

D.   I, II, and III

48.   When you give students a piece of writing that uses the third person and have them change it to first person, they will be practicing the element of the writing process called

A.   point of view.

B.   delimiting the topic.

C.   constructing a thesis.

D.   selecting the tense.

49.   Effective responses to students' writing include all of the following **EXCEPT**

A.   I liked the way you made the protagonist's intentions clear.

B.   Your point of view was perfectly appropriate for this piece.

C.   This is very good writing.

D.   The twists and turns in your plot would maintain the reader's interest.

50. Teachers should respond to student's writing by doing which of the following?

    A. Providing positive reinforcement by stating what was done well

    B. Calling attention to parts of the writing that need improvement

    C. Having the students focus their attention on the work of a peer and how it could be improved

    D. Asking students what they disliked most about their writing

51. Appropriate ways to assess students' writing include all of the following **EXCEPT**

    A. conduct a teacher-student writing conference.

    B. have the students keep individual tracking sheets on which they include comments about the quality of their writing.

    C. have the students use writing comment sheets which have sections for both student and teacher comments on the writing.

    D. use a highlighter to indicate all of the errors the student has made in his writing.

52. When two different words share the same or similar meaning, they are

    A. obsequies.

    B. onomatopoeias.

    C. homophones.

    D. synonyms.

53. According to the National Institute for Literacy, parents and educators "can encourage indirect vocabulary learning by first

    A. reading aloud to children, regardless of age or grade level."

    B. showing pictures to your children and mimicking the sounds associated with those pictures."

    C. allowing children to watch television shows designed to promote juvenile learning."

    D. exposing infants and very young children to classical music."

54. What is the definition of *literacy*?

    A.   a good thing for children to establish early in life

    B.   is essential to functioning well in a wide variety of situations

    C.   the ability to write prose and poetry in a manner that listeners and readers find pleasing

    D.   the ability to comprehend what one reads and writes

55. When paraphrasing the plot of a literary work, it is standard practice to

    A.   avoid any reference to tenses in your summarization.

    B.   summarize the piece in as few words as possible.

    C.   summarize the piece in chronological order.

    D.   summarize the piece in the present tense.

56. In a composition on literary analysis, where is the most appropriate spot to place the author's name, the title of the piece, and the thesis or central theme of your paper?

    A.   in the last sentence of the first paragraph

    B.   in the first sentence of the first paragraph

    C.   in the last sentence of the conclusion

    D.   in the first sentence of the conclusion

57. One of the most effective ways for readers to "engage" with the text is to

    A.   use a brightly colored highlighter to mark the significant passages.

    B.   read the entire author's works and the corresponding criticisms.

    C.   annotate the text with a pencil or pen and not highlighter.

    D.   read the entire text and then reflect on its thematic representation(s).

58. Why should children be taught to use graphic organizers as a method of organizing data during an inquiry?

 A. It discourages the practice of copying paragraphs out of the source book.

 B. It helps children to see similarities and differences across sources.

 C. Graphic organizers look good to parents.

 D. It provides the students an opportunity to use a word processor.

59. Why should children be encouraged to figure out the structure and the features of the text they are attempting to comprehend and remember?

 I. It helps the students to understand the way the author organized the material to be presented.

 II. It helps the students to really look at the features of the text.

 III. Talking about the structure of the text provides an opportunity for the teacher to point out the most salient features to the students.

 IV. The discussions may help the child make connections between the new material in the chapter and what is already known about the topic.

 A. I and III

 B. II and IV

 C. I and IV

 D. I, II, III, and IV

60. Having students make a semantic web of several books, including things such as the setting, the plot, and the characterization, is a good way to teach them

 A. the elements of the genre: the novel.

 B. the elements of the genre: the fable.

 C. the elements of the genre: the folktale.

 D. the elements of the genre: biography.

61. In their use of a dictionary, the most common weakness that youngsters demonstrate is their failure to

   A. know alphabetical order.

   B. use guide words to locate the word of interest.

   C. correctly spell the word of interest.

   D. locate the word of interest.

62. If youngsters need to locate specific information about an individual, the most appropriate reference book for them to use would be

   A. an almanac.

   B. an encyclopedia.

   C. a biographical dictionary.

   D. an atlas.

63. Students who use metacognition to enhance their reading comprehension have teachers who encourage them to

   I.   activate prior knowledge.

   II. make predictions.

   III. ask questions while reading.

   IV. summarize what they have read.

   A. I and III

   B. II, III, and IV

   C. I, II, and III

   D. I, II, III, and IV

64. A quickly and easily made assessment tool that teachers can make to assess strengths and weaknesses in students' reading is

   A. a checklist.

   B. a rubric.

   C. a running record.

   D. an anecdotal record.

65. Another name for an IRI (Informal Reading Inventory) is

    A. a running record.

    B. a miscue analysis.

    C. an anecdotal record.

    D. a dedicated checklist.

66. All of the following are examples of literary genre **EXCEPT**

    A. historical fiction.

    B. Victorian gothic.

    C. science fiction.

    D. realistic fiction.

67. Context clues should be taught in categories. Which of the following are categories of context clues?

    A. definitions of more complex or unusual words

    B. giving an example of what the word means

    C. comparison of the more difficult word with something more familiar

    D. all of the above

68. If an author portrays a character as having an "Achilles' heel" to refer to the character's weakness, he has used a literary device known as an

    A. allusion.

    B. idiosyncrasy.

    C. ideograph.

    D. illusionary.

69. Which of the following are appropriate strategies for teaching literature?

    I. creating plot diagrams

    II. rewriting the book's ending

    III. reading the book twice

    IV. designing a jacket or cover for the book

A. I, II, and III

B. I, II and IV

C. II, III, and IV

D. I, III, and IV

70. Which genre would most likely assist young adults with personal, social, and emotional development?

A. historical fiction

B. biography

C. realistic contemporary fiction

D. romantic fiction

71. Literature circles come together for the specific purpose of doing which of the following?

A. critiquing peers' choice of leisure books

B. discussing a designated book, author, or literary genre

C. discussing what book the class will read next

D. discussing books to recommend to friends

72. Persuasive speakers use which of the following approaches to convince their audience to agree with them?

    I. appeal to reason

    II. appeal to emotions

    III. appeal of coercion

    IV. appeal to character

A. I, II, and III

B. II, III, and IV

C. I, II, and IV

D. I, III, and IV

73. Someone listening to music while driving is engaged in what level or type of listening?

    A. attentive

    B. appreciative

    C. marginal

    D. analytical

74. Advertisers often use euphemisms in their commercials. Which of the following are euphemisms?

    I.   passed away

    II. faux diamond

    III. imitation leather

    IV. fresh off the tree

    A. I, II, and III

    B. II, III, and IV

    C. I, III, and IV

    D. I, II, and IV

75. A teacher videotaped several television commercials. The students were asked to decipher the real message the advertiser was sending. The teacher did this in order to make the students

    A. better viewers.

    B. critical consumers.

    C. better listeners.

    D. happy to watch television in school.

76. A teacher is giving oral directions to her class so that they can create a craft project. The teacher's goal is to assess the students'

    A. artistic ability.

    B. creativity.

    C. listening ability.

    D. interest in the project.

77. Having students view a film based on a book they have read and compare the two versions, helps them to become

   A.   better listeners.
   B.   film critics.
   C.   informed viewers.
   D.   better readers.

78. Assessment of speaking should

   I.   be performance-based in authentic contexts.
   II. include skills such as making eye contact.
   III. include the ability to stick to the subject.
   IV. include responding appropriately to audience questions.

   A.   I, II, and III
   B.   II, III, and IV
   C.   I, III, and IV
   D.   I, II, III, and IV

79. Today's students need to access computers. Drawbacks concerning the use of this technology in schools include which of the following?

   I.   Computers are difficult to use and require expertise.
   II. Computers are very expensive.
   III. Computers grow obsolete quickly and need to be replaced.
   IV. Computers should not become an end in and of themselves.

   A.   I, II, and III
   B.   II, III, and IV
   C.   I, II, and IV
   D.   I, II, III, and IV

80. Which of the following language arts are considered expressive?

        I.   speaking

        II. reading

        III. writing

        IV. listening

  A.   I and II

  B.   II and III

  C.   III and IV

  D.   I and III

81. Which of the following is an appropriate strategy that integrates math and writing?

  A.   Have students transcribe math word problems.

  B.   Have youngsters write their answers to math problems using words.

  C.   Have students write out step-by-step instructions for solving word problems

  D.   Have youngsters write out a complete explanation of their solution to a math problem.

82. Which of the following are cooperative learning strategies?

        I.   Puzzles

        II. Think-Pair-Share

        III. Numbered Heads Together

        IV. Jigsaw

  A.   I, II, and III

  B.   I, III, and IV

  C.   II, III, and IV

  D.   I, II, III, and IV

83. Which of the following activities would be appropriate for an integrated unit on World War II?

    I.   studying a map of the countries involved

    II. making a graph of the troop losses on each side

    III. interviewing veterans about their experiences

    IV. reading about the topic in a history textbook

  A. I, II, III, and IV

  B. I, II, and III

  C. II, III, and IV

  D. I, II, and IV

84. The lesson plan for an integrated lesson differs from that of a lesson in a single subject in which of the following ways?

  A. The lesson objectives are combined into a single statement of purpose.

  B. The procedures section includes activities in several curriculum areas.

  C. The assessment section combines all of the objectives into one global evaluation.

  D. The materials list is always more lengthy.

85. Which of the following are considered receptive language arts?

  A. speaking, reading, and listening

  B. viewing, listening, and reading

  C. listening, speaking, and viewing

  D. visually representing, listening, and reading

ESSAY ITEM

Assignment

Write a critical essay in which you respond to the following poem. The essay must include

- identification of theme;

- analysis noting literary techniques, including genre features, literary elements, and rhetorical devices used to express the theme; and

- a conclusion.

The Chimney Sweeper

When my mother died, I was very young,
And my father sold me while yet my tongue
Could scarcely cry 'weep! 'weep! 'weep! 'weep!'
So your chimneys I sweep, and in soot I sleep.

There's a little Tom Dacre, who cried when his head,
That curled like a lamb's back, was shaved: so I said,
"Hush, Tom! never mind it, for when your head's bare,
You know that the soot cannot spoil your white hair."

And so he was quiet; and that very night,
As Tom was a-sleeping, he had such a sight,
That thousands of sweepers, Dick, Joe, Ned, and Jack,
Were all of them locked up in coffins of black.

And by came an angel who had a bright key,
And he opened the coffins and set them all free;
Then down a green plain leaping, laughing, they run,
And wash in a river, and shine in the sun.

Then naked and white, all their bags left behind,
They rise upon clouds and sport in the wind;
And the angel told Tom, if he'd be a good boy,
He'd have God for his father, and never want joy.

And so Tom awoke; and we rose in the dark,
And got with our bags and our brushes to work,
Though the morning was cold, Tom was happy and warm;
So if all do their duty they need not fear harm.

William Blake, *Songs on Innocence*, 1789

ANSWER KEY—PRACTICE TEST 1

Question	Answer	Competency
1	D	Knowledge of the English Language
2	C	Knowledge of the English Language
3	B	Knowledge of Literature
4	A	Knowledge of Literature
5	C	Knowledge of Literature
6	C	Knowledge of the Reading Process to Construct Meaning
7	D	Knowledge of Literature
8	C	Knowledge of the English Language
9	A	Knowledge of the English Language
10	A	Knowledge of the English Language
11	B	Knowledge of the English Language
12	C	Knowledge of the Reading Process to Construct Meaning
13	D	Knowledge of the Reading Process to Construct Meaning
14	A	Knowledge of the Reading Process to Construct Meaning
15	D	Knowledge of the Reading Process to Construct Meaning
16	B	Knowledge of Literature
17	D	Knowledge of Literature
18	C	Knowledge of Literature
19	C	Knowledge of Literature
20	A	Knowledge of the English Language
21	C	Knowledge of the English Language
22	D	Knowledge of the English Language
23	A	Knowledge of Writing
24	C	Knowledge of Listening, Viewing, and Speaking
25	B	Knowledge of Listening, Viewing, and Speaking

Question	Answer	Competency
26	C	Knowledge of Listening, Viewing, and Speaking
27	C	Knowledge of the Reading Process to Construct Meaning
28	B	Knowledge of Listening, Viewing, and Speaking
29	D	Knowledge of the Reading Process to Construct Meaning
30	C	Knowledge of the Reading Process to Construct Meaning
31	B	Knowledge of Listening, Viewing, and Speaking
32	C	Knowledge of the English Language
33	C	Knowledge of the English Language
34	B	Knowledge of Writing
35	A	Knowledge of Writing
36	B	Knowledge of Writing
37	D	Knowledge of the English Language
38	B	Knowledge of the English Language
39	B	Knowledge of the English Language
40	B	Knowledge of the English Language
41	D	Knowledge of Listening, Viewing, and Speaking
42	B	Knowledge of Writing
43	C	Knowledge of the English Language
44	A	Knowledge of the English Language
45	A	Knowledge of Literature
46	A	Knowledge of Writing
47	C	Knowledge of Writing
48	A	Knowledge of Writing
49	C	Knowledge of Writing
50	A	Knowledge of Writing
51	D	Knowledge of Writing
52	D	Knowledge of the English Language
53	A	Knowledge of Listening, Viewing, and Speaking

Question	Answer	Competency
54	D	Knowledge of the Reading Process to Construct Meaning
55	D	Knowledge of Literature
56	B	Knowledge of Writing
57	C	Knowledge of the Reading Process to Construct Meaning
58	B	Knowledge of Writing
59	D	Knowledge of the Reading Process to Construct Meaning
60	A	Knowledge of the Reading Process to Construct Meaning
61	B	Knowledge of the English Language
62	C	Knowledge of the English Language
63	D	Knowledge of the Reading Process to Construct Meaning
64	A	Knowledge of the Reading Process to Construct Meaning
65	B	Knowledge of the Reading Process to Construct Meaning
66	B	Knowledge of Literature
67	D	Knowledge of the Reading Process to Construct Meaning
68	A	Knowledge of Literature
69	B	Knowledge of Literature
70	C	Knowledge of Literature
71	B	Knowledge of the Reading Process to Construct Meaning
72	C	Knowledge of Listening, Viewing, and Speaking
73	C	Knowledge of Listening, Viewing, and Speaking
74	A	Knowledge of Listening, Viewing, and Speaking
75	B	Knowledge of Listening, Viewing, and Speaking
76	C	Knowledge of Listening, Viewing, and Speaking
77	C	Knowledge of Listening, Viewing, and Speaking
78	D	Knowledge of Listening, Viewing, and Speaking
79	B	Knowledge of Listening, Viewing, and Speaking
80	D	Knowledge of Methods of Integration
81	D	Knowledge of Methods of Integration

Question	Answer	Competency
82	C	Knowledge of Methods of Integration
83	A	Knowledge of Methods of Integration
84	B	Knowledge of Methods of Integration
85	B	Knowledge of Methods of Integration

PRACTICE TEST 1 PROGRESS CHART

Knowledge of the English Language and Methods for Effective Teaching

16/20

1	2	8	9	10	11	20	21	22	32
					X				X

33	37	38	39	40	43	44	52	61	62
X									X

Knowledge of Writing and Methods for Effective Teaching

10/13

23	34	35	36	42	46	47	48	49
	X		X					

50	51	56	58
		X	

Knowledge of the Use of the Reading Process to Construct Meaning from a Wide Range of Selections

13/17

6	12	13	14	15	27	29	30	54
					X			

57	59	60	63	64	65	67	71
		X	X		X		

Knowledge of Literature and Methods for Effective Teaching

12/14

3	4	5	7	16	17	18	19	45	55
				X					X

66	68	69	70

Knowledge of Listening, Viewing, and Speaking as Methods for Acquiring Critical Literacy

13/15

24	25	26	28	31	41	53	72	73	74	75
	X									

76	77	78	79
		X	

Knowledge of the Methods for Integration of the Language Arts

5/6

80	81	82	83	84	85
			X		

Ability to Write Well on a Selection from Poetry or Prose, including Fiction or Nonfiction

—essay section

1. **D.**

   In a living language, words are added and others cease to be used.

2. **C.**

   The English language has changed due to the influences of history, new medical and scientific discoveries that have added vocabulary, and changes in social attitudes that have added vocabulary and changed the meanings of some words.

3. **B.**

   As being in nature is a cathartic experience to the Romantics, there needs to be a one-on-one relationship with no other distractions.

4. **A.**

   Think of realism as a literary attempt at photography—a realistic representation as opposed to a romantic one.

5. **C.**

   Scholars credit Homer, a Greek poet, with writing *The Iliad* and *The Odyssey*.

6. **C.**

   An effective persuasive argument must include a full recognition and clear analysis of the counterargument showing its strengths and weaknesses.

7. **D.**

   The association between Mark Twain and the Mississippi River is undeniable.

8. **C.**

   A topic sentence, usually located at the beginning of a paper, states the main premise of an essay.

9. **A.**

   According to the Oxford English Dictionary, *grammar* is defined as "the branch of language study or linguistic study which deals with the means of showing the relationship between words in use."

10. **A.**

    Transformational, traditional, and structural are legitimate approaches to teaching grammar; literal is not.

11. **B.**

    Alliteration means that a consonant sound at the beginning of a series of words is repeated.

12. **C.**

    Phrases such as "growing grim about the mouth" and "a damp, drizzly November in my soul" establish the passage's somber and melancholy tone.

13. **D.**

    The narrator means that if he doesn't get to the sea right away, he will kill himself. In other words, it suggests that sailing is the only cure for his depression.

14. **A.**

    The paragraph is written in a prosaic style, that is, having the characteristics of a prose narrative, as opposed to a poetic style and structure.

15. **D.**

    "A damp, drizzly November in my soul" is a metaphor, whereby symbols replace literal representations.

16. **B.**

    Old English, Middle English, Renaissance, Neoclassical, Romantic, Victorian, Modern periods.

17. **D.**

    Genre is a word of French that denotes the categorizing or classification of literary works by subject. Genres can include but are not limited to such categories as westerns, science fiction, horror, mystery, and detective stories.

18. **C.**

    The authors are all associated with the Romantic period.

19. **C.**

Mark Twain was the pen name for Samuel Langhorne Clemens, who took his pen name from the language of the river boats he so loved.

20. **A.**

A gerund is formed by adding –ing to a verb, resulting in a word that functions as a noun. For example, a verb like *swim* or *ski* becomes the name of the activity itself: He enjoys swimming, but skiing is his favorite sport.

21. **C.**

A run-on sentence is a sentence in which two or more independent clauses have been run together without a conjunction or proper punctuation.

22. **D.**

Infinitives—a verb plus the word *to*, as in *to go, to do,* and *to be*—avoid reference to time and thus are considered "infinite." For example, the sentence, "I am going to go to the store," could mean, "I'm on my way to the store now," or it could mean, "I will be going to the store some undesignated time in the future." A split infinitive is an infinitive in which an adverb or other modifier separates the *to* from the verb, as in *to boldly go*.

23. **A.**

There is a direct relationship between what is taught in school and what is learned in school. Also, if you want children to improve in writing, they need time to write.

24. **C.**

Clearly setting a purpose for listening, asking questions about the selection, and encouraging students to forge links between the new information and knowledge already in place are all supported by research as effective strategies.

25. **B.**

Through this question, a person will demonstrate his understanding of the difference between the concept of steady beat and the concept of rhythm. Answers (B) and (C) are both good answers, but the best answer is (B) because each of the syllables listed falls on a strong pulse (the beat) when spoken or sung. Answer (C) is made up of words that fall on the beat, but highlights larger segments encompassing multiple beats. Answer (D) highlights the beginnings of lines with no regard for the beat and answer (A) has no regard for the beat at all.

26. **C.**

Teaching effective comprehension is a process that takes time and practice. It seems obvious that a student cannot comprehend a text if the text cannot be decoded. It also seems obvious that, if you want students to get better at reading, they need time to read. Students also need time and input, usually in the form of conversation, to make connections between what is read and what is already known.

27. **C.**

The use of instructional strategies that make learning relevant to individual student interests is a powerful motivating force that facilitates learning and independent thinking. Choices (A) and (B) are both important factors to consider during a brainstorming session of this type, but both of these factors should influence the teacher only after the student interests have been included. Choice (D) indicates a misunderstanding of the situation described. The students are setting the objectives for the unit as they brainstorm questions.

28. **B.**

When trying to inform or teach, we are often intentionally repetitious to reinforce concepts.

29. **D.**

A scoring rubric is a grading form that includes each aspect of an assigned task and allows teachers to weight some aspects of the task, those which are more difficult, more highly than others.

30. **C.**

An IRI is primarily used to diagnose weaknesses in specific reading skills so that a teacher can target remediation. It can also indicate the student's instructional, independent, and frustration level, but this is not its primary purpose.

31. **B.**

It is important to distinguish between the skill of listening and the physical attribute of hearing.

32. **C.**

Research on the time it takes for second language learners to acquire Cognitive Academic Language Proficiency, if they are already literate in their native language, indicates that it takes from 5 to 7 years.

33. **C.**

    There would be no benefit derived by second language learners if teachers were to dictate to them in their second language and have them write it down. The other three strategies have all proven effective with ELL students.

34. **B.**

    Speaking precedes writing. Therefore, to develop proficient writers, one must first develop proficient speakers.

35. **A.**

    The authoring cycle consists of brainstorming ideas, making a rough draft, editing that rough draft, proofreading the draft, and making a final copy incorporating all of the changes.

36. **B.**

    A writing portfolio should be organized in chronological order so that improvement in writing over time is documented.

37. **D.**

    A metaphor is an example of figurative language.

38. **B.**

    Onomatopoeia is defined as a word that makes the sound of what it means.

39. **B.**

    Redundancy is defined as unnecessarily repeating oneself. It is already obvious that boiling water is hot, so saying that it is hot is redundant.

40. **B.**

    The word "gay" used to mean happy. In recent years, homosexual males have used this term to label themselves. Because of changes in the attitude of society toward homosexuals, this term is now used to mean this population.

41. **D.**

    A speaker needs to consider all of these factors in determining his use of language.

42. **B.**

   Back to the basics on this one: Active sentences put the subject of a sentence before the object, and passive sentences put the object of a sentence before the subject.

43. **C.**

   For a sentence to be complete, it must contain a noun or noun phrase, which serves as the sentence subject, and a verb or verb phrase, also known as the sentence's predicate. So, if a sentence's subject contains a noun phrase, then the sentence's predicate must contain a verb phrase.

44. **A.**

   The rule for applying a preposition or an article to all members of a series or list is that you must either use the preposition or article only before the first term, as in *the French, Italians, Spanish, and British,* or else the preposition or article must be repeated before every entry, as in *the French, the Italians, the Spanish, and the British.*

45. **A.**

   Answer (B) describes *allusion,* (C) describes a concrete word or phrase, and (D) is an erroneous example of ambiguous writing.

46. **A.**

   These are all activities that writers typically engage in during the prewriting or planning phase of writing.

47. **C.**

   These strategies would facilitate a student's choice of a writing topic. A prompt restricts the writer into responding and does not provide choice.

48. **A.**

   "Point of view" has to do with who is telling the story. Changing from first person, *I,* to third person, *you,* alters the perspective.

49. **C.**

   Giving students general feedback, such as saying that the writing is good, is not effective in terms of helping students improve their writing.

50. **A.**

    Positive reinforcement is far more effective than focusing on the negative.

51. **D.**

    Using a highlighter to indicate all the errors in a student's writing is focusing on the negative rather than the positive.

52. **D.**

    Various words that share the same or similar meaning, for example *city* and *metropolis,* are known as synonyms.

53. **A.**

    Reading aloud to your students, regardless of age or grade level, increases vocabulary. Reading aloud also augments comprehension when you discuss the selection with your students before, during, and after they read it.

54. **D.**

    Literacy is not simply the ability to read and write, but the ability to comprehend and/or process what one reads and writes.

55. **D.**

    When paraphrasing the plot of a literary work, it is standard practice to summarize the piece in the *present tense*—for example, "Friar Tuck *joins* Robin Hood's band"—rather than refer to the story and events in the past tense.

56. **B.**

    When writing a composition or response to a literary work, the most appropriate place to acknowledge the author's name, the title of the piece, and the central theme is in the first sentence of the essay.

57. **C.**

    One of the best ways for readers to engage with a text is to annotate the text with a pencil or pen, and not with a highlighter. At first this may seem contrary to popular practices, but highlighters simply mark words, while writing with a pen or pencil promotes active reading and thinking about the materials.

58. **B.**

Asking children to complete a graphic organizer as they research an issue helps them keep organized, see connections, and pull together what they can then use in some interesting and meaningful way.

59. **D.**

Children learn more from a text if the teacher helps them figure out how the book was put together. It makes the text more understandable. It also helps them to read the text critically, as part of the conversation can address the issue of what is missing in the text.

60. **A.**

Semantic webs pinpoint different aspects of a whole, in this case a novel. If youngsters make semantic webs for several novels, common attributes of this genre will become apparent.

61. **B.**

Observation of youngsters as they try to locate words in a dictionary quickly reveals that they fail to use the guide words correctly and search down entire pages to locate the word of interest.

62. **C.**

Youngsters should become familiar with specialized reference books such as biographical dictionaries.

63. **D.**

Metacognition relates to knowing what you know. Activating prior knowledge, making predictions, asking questions while reading, and summarizing what was read are all activities that facilitate comprehension.

64. **A.**

A checklist is quickly and easily constructed and can list reading skills so that it can be used to record a student's strengths and weaknesses. The other tools listed are far more involved and serve different purposes.

65. **B.**

An IRI is also referred to as a miscue analysis, as it is used to record the errors in decoding made by a student.

66. **B.**

Victorian gothic is a fabricated term; the others are generally accepted literary genres.

67. **D.**

Definitions, examples, and comparisons are all different kinds of context clues.

68. **A.**

An allusion is a literary device that is a reference to a well-known event, person, place, or literary work. Since Achilles' heel was this character's weak point, stating that a character has an Achilles' heel quickly makes this point clear.

69. **B.**

There is no virtue in reading a book twice except if the reader found it so enjoyable as to want to repeat the experience. The other activities are all appropriate for teaching literature.

70. **C.**

Realistic contemporary fiction usually deals with the same kinds of problems that young adults attempt to solve in their personal, social, and emotional development.

71. **B.**

This is the specific reason that literary circles are created.

72. **C.**

Persuasion involves the use of making an appeal to emotions, facts or reason, or character. Coercion does not constitute persuasion.

73. **C.**

If you are driving and listening to music, your attention is really on the driving and you are aware of the music, but it does not have much of your attention.

74. **A.**

A euphemism is a less direct or somewhat disguised way of saying something so that it is less hurtful. "Fresh off the tree" does not serve this purpose.

75. **B.**

   The teacher is clearly trying to aid her students in understanding advertising in order for them to become critical consumers.

76. **C.**

   One of the ways to assess listening is to see if students can follow oral directions.

77. **C.**

   Comparing a book and a film based on the book enables students to become informed viewers.

78. **D.**

   All of the attributes listed are generally seen as those belonging to an effective speaker.

79. **B.**

   Computers are not very difficult to use, but are expensive, do become obsolete quickly, and are sometimes allowed to become an end in and of themselves.

80. **D.**

   The expressive language arts are speaking, writing, and visually representing.

81. **D.**

   Students would incorporate math and writing skills jointly if they had to write an explanation to a math problem. The other choices don't accomplish both of these.

82. **C.**

   "Puzzles" is not the name of a cooperative learning strategy; the other three choices are.

83. **A.**

   A thematic unit on World War II should incorporate as many curriculum areas as appropriate. Incorporating social studies, math, listening, writing, and reading would all be appropriate for this unit.

84. **B.**

   An integrated lesson focuses on a variety of subjects. Therefore, the activities or procedures would involve several different curriculum areas.

85. **B.**

   The receptive language arts are reading, listening, and viewing.

ESSAY ITEM

Sample Responses

Seven-Point Response

   In William Blake's "The Chimney Sweeper," the images of a lonely child's misery, isolation, and suffering represent the Victorian philosophy that children were property to be used and then discarded when they outgrew their usefulness.

   In the poem, the young orphaned narrator expresses his misery with sounds of "weeping." At first, his crying is the result of the loss or abandonment of his parents, "my mother died . . . and my father sold me . . ." and "father and mother . . . both gone to the church to pray," and secondly by the harsh and dangerous labor, the "chimneys I sweep," he is required to perform. In addition, the fact that the narrator is very aware that his father "sold" him speaks to the issue of Victorian children as a viable commodity.

   At the same time that Blake paints the images of desolation, he presents his reader with the embodiment of death as in "coffins of black." The use of these references creates a somber atmosphere that reinforces the fact that the narrator who sleeps "in soot" lives in a blackened world filled with suffering and mortal danger, not allowing any chance for real rest.

   The author suggests a heavenly redemption where God and angels will watch the "thousand of sweepers" who have been set free as they are "leaping, laughing" and running "down a green plain." However, Blake returns to the reality of the cold morning and implies that this faith in impending redemption may be unwarranted.

   Overall, the poem's theme of the Victorian child's vulnerability and treatment as property are reinforced by the references to the child being "sold" into a dark and dangerous world, where he will know only sadness until his eventual death.

Five-Point Response

Blake describes Tom's dream in which he sees thousands of unnamed chimney sweeps such as himself, along with some specifically named sweeps, Dick, Joe, Ned, and Jack, "locked up in coffins of black." These images of the named children to whom the reader can relate, and the inclusion of a reference to "thousands" more who remain unnamed, which emphasizes the scope of the situation, suggest the author's view of this world as bleak and filled with despair and harsh conditions.

The references to the narrator's work of cleaning the chimneys and sleeping in soot provide the reader with a picture of child labor and exploitation during the industrial revolution in England.

Blake contrasts the actual desperate conditions with the "green plain" where the children were "leaping, laughing" and running in Tom's dream. In the dream, the angel promises Tom that he will find joy ("never want joy") in death.

Finally, the overall effect of the poem on the reader is to emphasize the deplorable conditions in England during the industrial revolution as portrayed by the orphaned narrator.

Three-Point Response

This is a very sad and depressing poem. It is depressing to read about the dirty chimneys that the boy is forced to clean and that his own father sold him after his mother died.

Blake says that Tom is "a good boy" who has to work rather than have fun by playing in the river and shining in the sun. Is Blake telling us that work is good for kids? Maybe he wants his reader to appreciate the value of a good day's work. Maybe he is trying to instill a work ethic.

Tom had his head shaved, but Blake doesn't explain why. He only makes sort of a joke of it by pointing out that his hair will not get dirty when he sleeps in the soot.

Blake seems to be telling us that hard work is good for kids and that they need to learn this in childhood. He is saying that while it is all right for them to dream about fun and games, the real world is not like that. He wants them to be good and work hard and then they will not have to worry about any harm coming to them.

One-Point Response

I think this poem is stupid and that it does not make very much sense. It is about working at a dirty, horrible job. If you do not like your job, you can always quit. I once had a boss who was very mean and one day he was mean and rude to me in front of the customers so I told him it wasn't nice to talk to me like that in front of the customers and he said I was fired, so I quit and then a week later I got another job of making stuffed bears at the mall. It wasn't hard, I just walked in and asked if they needed somebody and they said come back on Thursday and I got the job. So why doesn't Mr. Blake quit the job he doesn't like? He should just not go to work and go find another job instead. It's not hard making stuffed toys but sometimes it gets really busy and then we all get rushed but I take my time and do a good job on each one I make.

Sometimes bosses can be mean but some can be nice. I had one nice boss once and he liked the way I put the decorations in the window so he made me in charge of decorating the windows and he said I did a really good job. Once he even said that I made the display look like Macy's store window and I got embarrassed and laughed because I thought he was making fun of me until he told me that that was a good thing. So I got to do the store windows and one year at Christmas, I brought my friends over to see the windows I decorated and they all really liked it a lot and said it was really cool and I felt really good. So if Mr. Blake didn't like his job or his boss was really mean or rude to him or he just didn't like what he was doing then he could just quit and find a new job instead of complaining like he does in the poems.

Also he could ask his parents for help because parents are supposed to help their kids when they are in trouble or need money and such so why doesn't Mr. Blake just ask his parents for money? If he is a little kid than maybe he could do chores around the house or maybe he could mow lawns for the neighbors of something like that to earn extra money. You could get a paper route or something but then he'd have to get up early every morning and do it everyday even Christmas and New Year's day. But that's OK because my little brother did that until he got enough money for a new bike he wanted and he liked it even more because he got to earn it himself. Maybe Mr. Blake is so sad because he doesn't know how good it'd be for him to earn his own money and get what he wanted by working hard; but if his boss is just too mean or whatever than he should just quit going to his chimney job and find something else that he'd like to do better.

DETAILED EXPLANATION OF SCORES ON SAMPLE ESSAYS – PRACTICE TEST 1

Seven-Point Response

This response demonstrates clear and consistent understanding of the images in the poem being discussed. The writer has fully identified the theme as the Victorian view of children as commodities. In identifying the theme, the writer has pointed to the poet's use of imagery and descriptive vocabulary. In stating his position, the writer has made specific reference to the actual words used by the poet. The writer used the final paragraph to conclude his essay with a brief summary. Overall, the writer has written a well-organized essay that is clearly focused and shows a smooth progression of ideas. In doing so, he has used varied, appropriate, and accurate vocabulary.

Five-Point Response

This response demonstrates reasonably clear and consistent mastery by identifying the theme of the poem as instructed in the task. The writer used two references specific to the poem to support his argument that the world is bleak and filled with despair and harsh conditions. The writer concludes his essay but commenting on the overall effect of the poem rather than by actually summarizing his points in support of his thesis. The essay is well-organized and focused but does not delve as deeply into the subject as does the previous sample response that received a higher score. The ideas flow fairly well from one paragraph to the next and use somewhat varied vocabulary although not of the same quality as the higher rated sample.

Three-Point Response

In writing this response, the writer has clearly failed to grasp the message that the author is trying to send. The writer has not looked beyond the surface to get a sense of the true meaning of the poem. The writer raises a series of questions about what the poet might have intended, but offers no answers. The vocabulary used is not varied and not very sophisticated. The final paragraph, which should be used to summarize the writer's entire premise, instead offers a somewhat immature interpretation of only one part of the poem. In order to receive a higher score, the writer would have had to develop his position more effectively by discussing the theme of the poem in greater depth and by using additional examples in support of the premise.

One-Point Response

This response is rather juvenile and merely condemns the poem as "stupid." The writer also admits that he/she doesn't understand what the poet is trying to say. The writer takes a naïve view that the child who is the narrator of the poem should simply quit the job he doesn't like and find more agreeable work. The second and third paragraphs of this response stray so far from the task at hand, namely to discuss the theme of the poem and focus on how the poet communicated this to his reader, as to be almost ludicrous. The writer has used personal experiences far removed from those of the narrator in the poem. In addition, the writer has misused words, for example "than" instead of "then." There is also a lack of correct punctuation and the use of several run-on sentences. There is no true analysis of the real theme of the poem and no attempt to summarize the poet's intent in the last paragraph.

Practice Test 2

FTCE English 6–12

This test is also on CD-ROM in our special interactive FTCE English TEST*ware*®. It is highly recommended that you first take this exam on computer. You will then have the additional study features and benefits of enforced timed conditions and instantaneous, accurate scoring. See page 7 for guidance on how to get the most out of our FTCE English software.

ANSWER SHEET FOR PRACTICE TEST 2

1 _____	18 _____	35 _____	52 _____	69 _____
2 _____	19 _____	36 _____	53 _____	70 _____
3 _____	20 _____	37 _____	54 _____	71 _____
4 _____	21 _____	38 _____	55 _____	72 _____
5 _____	22 _____	39 _____	56 _____	73 _____
6 _____	23 _____	40 _____	57 _____	74 _____
7 _____	24 _____	41 _____	58 _____	75 _____
8 _____	25 _____	42 _____	59 _____	76 _____
9 _____	26 _____	43 _____	60 _____	77 _____
10 _____	27 _____	44 _____	61 _____	78 _____
11 _____	28 _____	45 _____	62 _____	79 _____
12 _____	29 _____	46 _____	63 _____	80 _____
13 _____	30 _____	47 _____	64 _____	81 _____
14 _____	31 _____	48 _____	65 _____	82 _____
15 _____	32 _____	49 _____	66 _____	83 _____
16 _____	33 _____	50 _____	67 _____	84 _____
17 _____	34 _____	51 _____	68 _____	85 _____

TIME: 1½ hours   85 questions
1 hour   1 essay question

1. Identify the problem in the following sentence: *I was on my way to the store for some supplies when my tire goes flat.*

    A. The sentence contains a dangling participle.

    B. The sentence has no clear referent and is thus a sentence fragment.

    C. The sentence contains an incorrect verb tense agreement.

    D. Inappropriate punctuation results in a comma splice.

2. The term *etymology* can be defined as

    A. the study of a word's origins, including its history and evolution.

    B. the study of a word's origins, including its meaning in a cultural context.

    C. the study of a word's history, including its relationship to another word.

    D. the study of the era in which a word entered the language.

Read the following excerpt from Franz Kafka's "A Hunger Artist" and then answer questions 3 and 4.

During these last decades, the interest in professional fasting has markedly diminished. It used to pay very well to stage such great performances under one's own management, but today that is quite impossible. We live in a different world now. At one time the whole town took a lively interest in the hunger artist; from day to day of his fast the excitement mounted; everybody wanted to see him at least once a day; there were people who bought season tickets for the last few days and sat from morning till night in front of his small barred cage; even in the nighttime there were visiting hours, when the whole effect was heightened with torch flames; on fine days the cage was set out in the open air, and then it was the children's special treat to see the hunger artist; for their elders he was often just a joke that happened to be in fashion, but the children stood open-mouthed, holding each other's hands for greater security, marveling at him as he sat there pallid in black tights, with his ribs sticking out so prominently, not even on a seat but down among the straw on the ground, sometimes giving a courteous nod, answering questions with a constrained smile, or perhaps stretching an arm through the bars so that one might feel how thin it was, and then again withdrawing deep into himself, paying no attention to anyone or anything, not even to the all-important striking of the clock that was the only piece of furniture in his cage, but merely staring into vacancy with half shut eyes, now and then taking a sip from a tiny glass of water to moisten his lips.

3. In this paragraph, Kafka is using hunger as a metaphor for

    A. oil, watercolor, and acrylic paints.

    B. organized religion and spirituality.

    C. nothing; he is talking about food.

    D. social courtesy and social propriety.

4. What do "grown-ups" often think of the hunger artist?

    A. that he is merely a joke

    B. that he is quality entertainment

    C. that he is a sensitive artist

    D. that he is lonely and confused

5. A heroic couplet consists of lines of iambic pentameter that rhyme in pairs: *aa, bb, cc*, and so on. Who is credited with the introduction of this poetic style?

    A. Homer

    B. William Shakespeare

    C. Sophocles

    D. Geoffrey Chaucer

6. A sonnet, whether Italian or English, is

    A. a lyric poem consisting of a single stanza of 14 lines of iambic pentameter linked by an intricate rhyme scheme.

    B. a lyric poem consisting of two stanzas of 12 lines of trochaic meter linked by an intricate rhyme scheme.

    C. an epic poem consisting of 14 lines of iambic pentameter linked by a free-flowing rhyme scheme.

    D. a Romantic poem consisting of a single stanza of 15 lines of iambic pentameter linked by an intricate rhyme scheme that ends in a heroic couplet.

7. A soliloquy is

    A. an extended medieval poem that follows a standardized *abab* rhyme scheme and comprises a character's reflections on the existence of God.

    B. a monologue in which a character speaks his or her thoughts and feelings aloud.

    C. a monologue in which a character confesses his or her innermost feelings to the person whom he or she loves.

    D. an extended dialogue between two principal characters, usually consisting of witty conversation and word play.

8. A metaphor is an example of

    A. literal interpretation.

    B. figurative language.

    C. logical fallacies.

    D. somnambulism.

9. T. S. Eliot's *The Waste Land* is a poetic example of

    A. modernism.

    B. lyricism.

    C. a ballad.

    D. an epic.

10. Many modern poets, such as Emily Dickinson, W. B. Yeats, William Blake, and Dylan Thomas deliberately supplement a perfect rhyme scheme with an imperfect or slant rhyme scheme. What is an imperfect, or slant, rhyme?

    A.   a rhyme scheme that is deliberately unfinished, or made to appear incomplete, usually for a dramatic or suspenseful effect

    B.   a rhyme scheme in which corresponding vowel sounds are only approximate, and sometimes the rhymed consonants are similar rather than identical

    C.   a rhyme scheme that represents a spontaneous overflowing of human emotions and thus seems hastily written or biased in its content

    D.   a rhyme scheme that intentionally sacrifices the lyrical rhyme scheme in order to emphasize the importance of its social or political content

11. Syntax is

    A.   a division of linguistics that studies synonyms.

    B.   the study of how words and their component parts combine to form sentences.

    C.   a physiological inability to form or comprehend coherent sentences.

    D.   the order and arrangement of words or symbols forming a logical sentence.

12. If an author states that a character's home reminds him of Noah's Ark because it has a lot of animals, the author is using a literary device called

    A.   alliteration.

    B.   analogy.

    C.   allusion.

    D.   allegory.

13. Reading which of the following might assist a young person's social development?

    A.   *The Bluest Eye* by Toni Morrison

    B.   *The Sound and the Fury* by William Faulkner

C. *The Call of the Wild* by Jack London

D. *The Crucible* by Arthur Miller

14. What is a morpheme?

    A. a word that combines other words and establishes its own meaning, as in *businessman* (*business* + *man*)

    B. a word that changes from a noun to a verb when *–ing* is added, as in *swim/swimming*

    C. a quantitative noun that changes spelling when going from singular to plural, as in *mouse/mice*

    D. the smallest unit of language that has meaning or serves a grammatical function, such as *cat*

15. An affix, also known as a bound morpheme,

    A. attaches to a word, thus giving it the opposite connotation from its original meaning; for example, *non-* added to *negotiable* creates the word *nonnegotiable*.

    B. attaches to a root or stem morpheme and can be either a prefix or a suffix.

    C. attaches to a verb, thereby making it an adverb; for example, *-ly* added to *swift* creates the adverb *swiftly*.

    D. attaches words with a hyphen, as in *nineteenth-century*.

16. What is a metaphor?

    A. a figure of speech containing an implied comparison in which a word or phrase ordinarily and primarily used for one thing is applied to another, as in "All the world's a stage."

    B. a figure of speech containing contemporary representation of linguistic ideology, primarily used by fiction writers, as in "That car is phat."

    C. a figure of speech containing a reproduction of the sounds that the word is supposed to represent, as in *buzz*

    D. a figure of speech containing the implied thematic representation of a story, fable, or morality tale, as in "Slow and steady wins the race."

17. Which of the following are appropriate interdisciplinary activities?

      I.   reading a book on the main topic

     II. using the Internet to research aspects of the topic

    III. making a chart to record data on the subject

    IV. writing to an authority on the subject seeking information

   A.   I, II, III, and IV

   B.   I, III, and IV

   C.   II, III, and IV

   D.   I, II, and IV

18. A colon tells the reader that what follows is closely related to the preceding clause. Which of the following sentences uses the colon correctly?

   A.   A dedicated artist: requires brushes, paint, a canvas, and an eye for beauty.

   B.   A dedicated artist requires four things: brushes, paint, a canvas, and an eye for beauty.

   C.   A dedicated artist requires materials such as paint: brushes: a canvas, and an eye for beauty.

   D.   A dedicated artist requires materials consisting of paint, brushes, a canvas: and an eye for beauty.

19. When a verbal phrase does not refer to a specific noun or noun phrase, it is known as a(an)

   A.   dangling modifier.

   B.   past participle.

   C.   predicate.

   D.   independent clause.

20. The following sentence has a dangling modifier: "Last night I shot an elephant in my pajamas." Which of the following sentences is the best correction of that error?

   A.   I shot an elephant last night.

   B.   An elephant was wearing my pajamas when I shot him.

C. Last night, while I was wearing my pajamas, I shot an elephant.

D. Elephants do not wear pajamas.

21. An important technique for proper literary assessment is to

A. have students read and reread various texts until they comprehend the symbolic representations.

B. have students articulate what they have read.

C. watch and document students, noting the ones who are eager to read.

D. watch students' performances in authentic learning situations.

22. An analysis or interpretation of a literary work involves

A. avoiding oversimplified plot and thematic summaries.

B. using oversimplified plot and thematic summaries.

C. facts and supporting materials taken from reliable secondary sources.

D. a brief, general outline of the author's literary credentials.

23. An integrated lesson differs from a traditional lesson in which of the following ways?

I. It always requires more materials to teach.

II. It always involves asking the students more questions.

III. It always involves more areas to assess.

IV. It always requires more time.

A. I and II

B. II only

C. III only

D. III and IV

24. *Literary naturalism* is best defined as

    A. a literary attempt to record accurately and objectively visual reality in terms of transient effects of light and color, thereby representing the various shapes and colors found in nature.

    B. giving the effect that the writing represents the nature of life and the social world as it seems to the common reader.

    C. the belief that every person exists entirely in the order of nature and does not have a soul or any participation in a religious or spiritual world beyond nature.

    D. the representation of the human condition based on loose and free-flowing designs, patterns, and shapes, like those found in nature.

25. Which of the following is the title of the autobiography of Booker T. Washington?

    A. *The Souls of Black Folk*

    B. *Uncle Tom's Cabin*

    C. *Yes, I Can*

    D. *Up from Slavery*

26. Which of the following statements best describes epic poetry, such as Homer's *The Iliad* and *The Odyssey?*

    A. an extended narrative poem based on the heroic exploits and/or extraordinary adventures of an individual involved in an extended quest

    B. an extended lyrical poem based on tribal values and religious ideologies of certain indigenous cultures

    C. an extended prosaic narrative whereby a group of individuals finds spiritual enlightenment through social and spiritual hardship and/or exaggerated strife

    D. a hyperbolic representation of the feats and actions of a real-life individual who has been characterized for fictional purposes

27. Sonnets and other forms of English poetry, such as Thomas Gray's "Elegy Written in a Country Churchyard," are written in iambic pentameter. What is iambic pentameter?

    A. five lines of poetry, with each line consisting of five stressed syllables followed by five light syllables

    B. five feet per line of one light syllable followed by a stressed syllable

    C. a poem limited to five stanzas, with each stanza limited to five lines

    D. one stressed syllable follow by a light syllable appearing in every fifth word per line

28. The term *alliteration* means which of the following?

    A. a repetitive vowel sound occurring at the beginning of a word or of a stressed syllable within a word

    B. a repetitive consonant sound occurring at the beginning of a word or of a stressed syllable within a word

    C. a repetitive vowel sound occurring at the end of a word or of a stressed syllable within a word

    D. a repetitive consonant sound occurring at the end of a word or of a stressed syllable within a word

29. What makes concrete poems, also known as pattern poems, unique from more conventional forms of poetry?

    A. Concrete poems avoid the use of figurative phrases and ambiguous language, using instead symbolic representations that are more literal and thus concrete.

    B. Concrete poems are structured around recurring refrains or poetic choruses, resulting in a poem that sounds more musical or melodic.

    C. Concrete poems are written in the visual shape of their textual content.

    D. Concrete poems were written at the beginning of the Industrial Revolution, lauding the sociopolitical benefits of steel and concrete.

Read the following sonnet by William Shakespeare and then answer questions 30 and 31.

Shall I compare thee to a summer's day?
Thou art more lovely and more temperate:
Rough winds do shake the darling buds of May,
And summer's lease hath all too short a date:
Sometime too hot the eye of heaven shines,
And often is his gold complexion dimm'd:
And every fair from fair sometime declines,
By chance or nature's changing course untrimm'd:
But thy eternal summer shall not fade
Nor lose possession of that fair thou owest;
Nor shall Death brag thou wand'rest in his shade,
When in eternal lines to time thou growest:
So long as men can breathe or eyes can see,
So long lives this and this gives life to thee.

30. All sonnets, whether Shakespearean or Petrarchan, contain a heroic couplet. In the sonnet you just read, which two lines make up the heroic couplet?

   A. "So long as men can breathe or eyes can see, / So long lives this and this gives life to thee"

   B. "Nor lose possession of that fair thou owest; / Nor shall Death brag thou wand'rest in his shade"

   C. "And often is his gold complexion dimm'd: / And every fair from fair sometime declines"

   D. "By chance or nature's changing course untrimm'd / But thy eternal summer shall not fade"

31. Which of the following statements best summarizes the theme of Shakespeare's sonnet?

   A. The metaphors relating to nature suggest that love is a part of nature (a naturally occurring phenomenon of the natural world) and therefore, like nature itself, transcends death, existing eternally.

B. The phrases "Rough winds do shake," "nature's changing course untrimm'd," and "Death brag thou wand'rest in his shade" suggest a tempestuous theme, one of a love relationship that is both difficult and challenging but perhaps ultimately worth the effort.

C. The narrator's hurried tone and references to the passing of time suggest, like Marvell's enamored plea in "To His Coy Mistress," the theme of *carpe diem*, or the need to hurry up and "seize the day" when it comes to love and intimacy.

D. The poet's use of extended apostrophe suggests a self-conscious artistic endeavor whereby the theme is one of aesthetic ability rather than the conceptual theme of love and relationships.

32. Novels that accentuate elements of medieval castles, dungeons, hidden passages with hidden chambers, and the exploits of a sexually perverse, sadistic villain trying to impose himself on an innocent young maiden are more commonly referred to as

A. grotesque novels.

B. episodic novels.

C. gothic novels.

D. epistolary novels.

33. Every successful college essay needs a clear, coherent thesis. What is a working thesis?

A. a single solidified idea stated as an assertion in response to a question

B. a general idea that guides the writing of the essay but will be refined during the writing process

C. a "road map" that guides the reader to the topic and content of the essay

D. an idea that fits the topic or works well in addressing the assigned question-at-issue

34. In the mid-1800s English artisans, including Dante Gabriel Rossetti and his sister Christina, formed a group that attempted to "return to the truthfulness, simplicity, and spirit of art, prior to the early Italian Renaissance." This "brotherhood" is more commonly known as the

   A.   Gregorian poets.

   B.   feudal poets.

   C.   Pre-Raphaelite poets.

   D.   Romantic poets.

35. What is a mother tongue?

   A.   language skills acquired from the maternal (mother's) side of a person's family

   B.   the first language a person learns—that is, the person's native language

   C.   the accepted language of the area or region where a person lives

   D.   the Latin base from which our modern-day languages developed

36. In the sentence "Pull gently on an old rope," the word *gently* is

   A.   a noun.

   B.   a verb.

   C.   an adjective.

   D.   an adverb.

37. What must a sentence contain for it to be considered a complete sentence?

   A.   a predicate and a claim

   B.   a noun and a verb

   C.   a verb and an adjective

   D.   a noun and an adjective

38. Thomas Gray's "Elegy Written in a Country Churchyard" (1751) is considered by many scholars as the definitive masterpiece of what school of poets and poetry?

    A.   graveyard

    B.   Pre-Raphaelite

    C.   Homeric

    D.   Romantic

39. What is the definition of *paragraph*?

    A.   a group of sentences that develop the various aspects of certain ideas or claims

    B.   a group of sentences that express the author's emotional response to an issue

    C.   a group of sentences that develop one main (complete) idea

    D.   a group of sentences that express the contemporary views of a society

40. When a writer chooses between words like *was/were, have/had/has,* or *run/ran,* that writer is actually selecting the appropriate

    A.   gendered nouns.

    B.   extraneous adjectives.

    C.   proper nouns.

    D.   verb tense.

41. Which of the following terms means "a word used to modify, or qualify a verb, an adjective, or another adverb"?

    A.   adverb

    B.   noun

    C.   adjective

    D.   verb

42. Paraphrasing is an essential component in the construction of an essay. What is the definition of *paraphrasing*?

    A. duplicating the argumentative phrasing twice in strategic locations within the essay

    B. restating a text or thesis in your own words, thereby making the idea or topic clearer to understand

    C. using two parallel symbols to suggest that the argument or textual idea is malleable and therefore subject to scrutiny

    D. replacing the author's name with your own and taking credit for the work that author produced

43. When a student has difficulty with reading retention, the recommended procedure for improving retention skills would include

    A. using classroom materials that are designated for lower grade levels and thus are less intimidating.

    B. increasing the amount of time the student spends on repetition and review.

    C. reading aloud, slowly and clearly, articulating as many words as possible.

    D. designating the student as developmentally disabled and referring him or her to counseling.

44. In 1999, a long-term study by the National Assessment of Educational Programs found a positive relationship between children's reading scores and

    A. the economic income levels of their parents.

    B. the social standings of their parents.

    C. the ethnic origins of their parents.

    D. the educational levels of their parents.

45. A word that shares phonetic similarities with another word, as in *sea* and *see,* is commonly known as

    A. an acronym.

    B. a Dictaphone.

C.   a homophone.

D.   a synonym.

46. Which of the following is the best example of onomatopoeia?

A.   ha-ha, whip, hop, hope

B.   sneeze, cough, laugh, blink

C.   buzz, hiss, whoosh, ding-dong

D.   zip, bump, jump, stump

47. Which of the following sentences contains a dangling modifier?

A.   Maria watched TV all night long.

B.   After completing the course on grammar, Ian's essays showed great improvement.

C.   Jake had no idea which direction to choose.

D.   Keiko wanted dinner, but her brother Elmo was not hungry yet.

48. Although the term *morphology* can pertain to a field of biological study, it is also a branch of linguistic study. What is morphology?

A.   the study of the fundamental structure and formation of words, including inflection, derivation, and the formation of compound words

B.   the study of an indigenous culture's ability to assimilate or adapt various sounds and vocal patterns into its own vocabulary

C.   the study of ancient tablets, codices, and scrolls for the purpose of understanding the evolution of language over an extended period

D.   the study of the ancient scribes who constructed alphabets and translated text for the illiterate, as they provided "modern" writing structures and fundaments still in use today

49. The origin of our modern English language is

    A.   Latin.

    B.   Greek.

    C.   Germanic.

    D.   Roman.

Read the following story and then answer questions 50 through 54.

I began my days as a cow. Well, a calf, to be more precise. I was born to the world a soft, tawny color, with liquid brown eyes and soft, floppy ears that begged to be touched. My days were simple. I spent all my time in the company of other bovine females, most especially my mother. She was a prized breeder, my mother; as a result, it was my misfortune to be weaned earlier than most other calves.

Only hours after my weaning, a miraculous event changed the course of my life. Princess Georgette happened to be riding by on her shaggy little pony, alongside her nanny, when she heard my lows of despair and turned.

"Whatever could be making that pitiful noise?" she asked aloud.

One of the farmers called out to her, "'Tis only a wee calf, Highness. She'll not be at it long, I assure you."

"I shall see the creature at once," she ordered, pulling her pony up against the rail and dismounting.

At this point, I had moved hopefully toward the commotion, and, as I inched my tender nose out of the barn to investigate, I came face to face with the oddest-looking creature I had seen so far in my somewhat short existence. She had outrageous red curls rioting all over her head and tumbling down over her shoulders. The thing I noticed most, though, was her hopelessly freckled nose, which, at that moment, was uncomfortably close to my own—so close, in fact, that I decided to remedy my discomfort and did so by lowing rather loudly in her petulant little face. To my astonishment, she giggled with delight at my rudeness, and reached out to stroke my furry forehead. I found myself nuzzling up to her small chest. "Oh Nan, I must have it. Such a funny furry thing must be kept in my garden where I might entertain myself endlessly with it."

So that is how I became a member of the royal household.

My days fell into an odd sort of routine. I spent my mornings cropping the lawns and shrubs until Georgette would appear, luring me into the hedge ways with a handful of cresses nipped from the kitchen. As soon as I got close enough and started to nibble, she would shriek, and startle me into a canter, at which point she would chase me into the hedges until I was so thoroughly lost, I would have to low helplessly until Georgette found me.

Tragically, calves do not stay calves forever. As the seasons passed, her interest in our games began to wane. The gardeners had, at this time, gotten very tired of working around me as I lumbered through the hedges. They communicated up through the chain of command, straight to the king himself, their wish to be rid of me. He dismissed the problem with an order to have me put down.

Georgette pouted at this and stamped her foot, but her father would not budge an inch. "Now, don't get missish with me, Georgette. I've given the order, and I'll see it done as I've dictated whether you like it or not."

Georgette, during this speech, had become thoughtful. After a long pause, she proposed, "Well, if I must see my Bessie put down as you've said, mightn't I get a handbag and boots out of her at least?"

"Very well," sighed her father.

For my part, it was a stroke of luck that this conversation had taken place just on the other side of the hedge where I had been, only moments before, contentedly munching on the last bit of clover to be found this season. Naturally, I took exception to being discussed in such a candid manner. In fact, I could not believe my furry, floppy ears. I felt myself slipping into a sort of self-pity and walked away. When I passed the westernmost gate, it occurred to me that I might not have to face my doom. This door, which was normally latched and guarded, stood open. I was out that gate and on the lane nearby in an instant.

I wandered aimlessly for hours, when I abruptly came upon a little clearing. A stream ran through it, past the coziest of tiny cottages. I trotted straight over to the stream and began drinking in long draughts. After several moments of such behavior, I became aware of another presence nearby. It was a small old man, leaning toward me in a strange sort of furry robe, balancing himself on the most incredibly gnarled staff and holding a silver bucket that steamed and hissed yet smelled overwhelmingly delicious.

"Hello," he said in a pleasant tone. "I'm happy you have finally arrived. I read it in *The Book*. Would you care to drink from my bucket?" he asked.

50. This is the beginning of a story. To what genre does it belong?

    A. poetry

    B. historical fiction

    C. nonfiction

    D. fantasy

51. What is likely to happen next?

    A. Bessie will go to a barn.

    B. Bessie will catch frogs.

    C. Bessie will run away.

    D. Bessie will drink the potion and turn into a brown-eyed girl.

52. How did you know what might happen next?

    A. The nanny never wanted the princess to have a pet cow in the first place.

    B. Magical things often happen in stories that begin with a princess.

    C. I have read about dysfunctional families.

    D. The king had ordered that Bessie be put down.

53. How should this sort of story be introduced to students?

    A. complete a K-W-L to activate prior knowledge about fairy tales

    B. ask the students to look up vocabulary words in a dictionary

    C. read the children a nonfiction book about dairy farming

    D. show a video about talking to strangers

54. If you were going to ask the students to finish this story as a writing activity, what would you do next?

    A. have them complete a worksheet about the vocabulary words

B.   ask them to diagram the first sentence

C.   ask them to form small groups in which they discuss what might happen next

D.   have them complete a Venn diagram about Bessie and a real cow

55.   Dr. Kenneth Goodman developed the notion of miscue analysis. It is a system for examining how a youngster's oral reading of a passage varies from

A.   singing the same passage.

B.   encoding the passage from a dictation.

C.   the printed text.

D.   diagrams of the sentences.

56.   Before reading a story to the students, Mrs. Drake tells the students what she is expecting them to learn from listening to the story. What is her reason for doing that?

A.   The students should know why the instructor chose that text over any other.

B.   It is important for teachers to share personal ideas with their students to foster an environment of confidence and understanding.

C.   Mrs. Drake wants to verify that all students are on task before she begins the story.

D.   Mrs. Drake is modeling a vital prereading skill to teach it to the young readers.

57.   Which of the following are research tools?

I.   the library

II.   the Internet

III.   interviews

A.   I only

B.   I and II

C.   I and III

D.   I, II, and III

58. In teaching higher-level reading skills, Mr. Chin wants his students to recognize editorializing. Which of these best illustrates editorializing?

   A.   Robert McGee was given a well-deserved round of applause.

   B.   Also discussed at the board meeting was the condition of the South Street School.

   C.   The company received its charter in 1912.

   D.   Just before he sat down, Mr. McPherson asked, "Has the homework been completed?"

As part of a unit on literary genres, Mrs. Nemetski presents the class with the following story. Read the story and then answer question 59.

A fisherman was trying to lure fish to rise so that he could hook them. He took his bagpipes to the banks of the river and played them. No fish rose out of the water. Next he cast his net into the river, and when he brought it back, the net was filled with fish. Then he took up his bagpipes again, and as he played, the fish leaped up into the net.

"Ah, now you dance when I play," he said to an old fish.

"Yes," said the old one, "when you are in a person's power you must do as he commands."

59. To which genre does this story belong?

   A.   narrative

   B.   character analysis

   C.   editorial

   D.   fable

Read the following poem and then answer questions 60 through 62.

A flea and a fly in a flue
Were caught, so what could they do?
Said the fly, "Let us flee."
"Let us fly," said the flea.
So they flew through a flaw in the flue.

60. The poem is

    A.   an elegy.

    B.   a ballad.

    C.   a limerick.

    D.   haiku.

61. The repetition of *fl* in *flea, fly,* and *flue* is called

    A.   alliteration.

    B.   onomatopoeia.

    C.   imagery.

    D.   symbolism.

62. A follow-up activity for the poem might include

    I.   having students illustrate the poem.

    II.   asking students to write their own poem in the same form.

    III.   having students clap their hands to practice the rhythm of the poem.

    A.   I only

    B.   I and II

    C.   I and III

    D.   I, II, and III

63. The proverb "Death is a black camel that kneels at the gates of all" is an example of

    A.   alliteration.

    B.   simile.

    C.   metaphor.

    D.   hyperbole.

64. Mr. Brown is teaching his class how to recognize propaganda. He presents students with the slogan, "Buy a brand-new Whizzer bike like the ones all your friends have." Which propaganda device is he illustrating?

    A. bandwagon

    B. testimonial

    C. card stacking

    D. glittering generality

65. Mrs. Blanchard uses a strategy in which she has her students copy key words from the board and listen to cue words that reinforce the key words. Next, the students write down information about the key words using lines as bullets. Then, the students write down questions the teacher presents and the answers to those questions. Next, the students read the textbook at home and try to find the key concepts discussed in class. Finally, those concepts are written in the students' own words in their notebooks. Which skill is Mrs. Blanchard trying to reinforce by using this method?

    A. creative writing

    B. organizational strategies

    C. note taking

    D. comprehension of a textbook chapter

66. Which author wrote, "What's in a name? That which we call a rose / By any other name would smell as sweet"?

    A. Christopher Marlowe

    B. Ben Johnson

    C. William Shakespeare

    D. Geoffrey Chaucer

67. Which line on the following chart best matches the resources with the historical research question being asked?

Line	Historical Research Question	Source of Information
1	How many people were living in Boston, Massachusetts, during the time of the American Revolution?	Historical atlas
2	What role did Fort Mackinac fulfill during the American Revolution?	Encyclopedia
3	How did the average temperatures and snowfall during the winter of 1775–76 compare with previous winters?	Historical almanac
4	When was the first U.S. treaty signed, and what were the terms of the treaty?	Diary of a participant

- A. line 1
- B. line 2
- C. line 3
- D. line 4

Read the following passage, written in the style of a newspaper editorial, and then answer questions 68 through 71.

[1]The zoning regulations of Westtown have long been a thorn in the side of local real estate developers. [2]The authors of those regulations apparently believed that their regulations would be appropriate in perpetuity, because they _____ to amend. [3]The result is a growing area of blight bounded on the north by Bradley Avenue and on the east by Randolph Street.

[4]This coming Wednesday the Westtown's city council has a chance to bring its zoning practices into the twenty-first century. [5]The decisive votes will come from councilmembers Putman, Beckett, and Reis. [6]The votes of Putman and Beckett in particular will be of interest to their constituents, because the residents of their wards would stand to gain a great deal from rezoning. [7]The proposed changes would bring the Fourth Ward some much-needed commerce in the currently run-down Randolph-Mackenzie area and would help _____ the Fifth Ward's steady population loss. [8]Although each of these self-styled "progressives" have displayed reluctance to vote for anything that would spur

development in the recent past, both have strong opposition in the upcoming election and would do well to consider how their votes on this issue will impact the results of that election.

68. Which of the following changes is needed in the passage above?

   A.   part 1: change *have* to *has*

   B.   part 4: change *Westtown's* to *Westtown*

   C.   part 8: change the comma after *past* to a semicolon

   D.   part 8: change *how* to *that*

69. Which of the following words would be the best to insert into the blank in part 7?

   A.   alleviate

   B.   accelerate

   C.   excoriate

   D.   exonerate

70. Which of the numbered parts should be revised to correct an error in verb form?

   A.   part 3

   B.   part 5

   C.   part 6

   D.   part 8

71. Which of the following phrases, inserted into the blank in part 2, would make sense and be free of errors?

   A.   made the regulations very easy

   B.   ensured that the provisions would be difficult

   C.   made them almost impossible

   D.   said the zoning ordinances will be hard

72. If a student's purpose is to give a persuasive speech, she or he is likely to

      I.   use factual information.

      II. appeal to character.

      III. appeal to snobbery.

      IV. appeal to emotions.

  A.   I, II, and IV

  B.   I, II, III, and IV

  C.   II, III, and IV

  D.   I, III, and IV

73. Which of the following assessment tools requires a teacher to observe a student and record, as soon as possible afterward, an account of exactly what took place?

  A.   a running record

  B.   an anecdotal record

  C.   an informal reading inventory

  D.   a scene account

74. A supportive classroom environment for writing includes

      I.   the formation of a community of writers.

      II. scheduled writing days and times.

      III. writing portfolios.

      IV. time to share and discuss writing.

  A.   I, II, and IV

  B.   II, III, and IV

  C.   I, II, III, and IV

  D.   I, III, and IV

75. Effective responses to student writing include which of the following?

   I. praising students' writing by saying, "Good work"

   II. asking students to indicate what they like best about a particular piece of writing

   III. asking students to determine if they have been successful in addressing the intended audience

   IV. having students select pieces of writing to include in their portfolios, based on improvement, and attaching a comment card to each piece that indicates the specific reason the piece was chosen

   A. I, II, and III

   B. I, III, and IV

   C. II, III, and IV

   D. I, II, and IV

76. Student writing can be assessed effectively by all the following **EXCEPT**

   A. a conference between the student and his or her peers.

   B. having the student complete a checklist indicating the behaviors in which she or he engaged during each step in the writing process.

   C. having the student keep a writing log.

   D. having the teacher circle all the errors in the piece.

77. Which of the following are appropriate strategies for teaching literature?

   I. having students write their own books

   II. having artistic students create a book jacket for a book they have read

   III. having students write a letter to a contemporary author about the inspiration for the book

   IV. after reading a historical fiction work, having students research the actual events on which the book is based and compare them with the events related in the book

A. I, II, and IV

B. I, II, III, and IV

C. II, III, and IV

D. I, III, and IV

78. The types of public speaking that usually include a moderator are which of the following?

      I. conversation

      II. panel discussion

      III. debate

      IV. Reader's Theater

A. I and II

B. II and III

C. III and IV

D. I and IV

79. A teacher is giving students a series of instructions to follow. Which level of listening is the teacher evaluating?

A. marginal

B. appreciative

C. attentive

D. analytical

80. Several outstanding, well-known professional athletes appear in advertisements for a diet plan that they say helped them to lose weight. This approach to advertising is categorized as

A. glittering generalities.

B. bandwagon.

C. testimonial.

D. doublespeak.

81. Students need to become aware of the intended effects of media. Among the common effects are

    I.   entertaining.

    II. persuading.

    III. joking.

    IV. informing.

    A. I, II, and III

    B. II, III, and IV

    C. I, III, and IV

    D. I, II, and IV

82. Which of the following strategies are appropriate for assessing a visual?

    I.   asking for the main idea of the visual

    II. asking fact-based questions

    III. having students define words used in the visual

    IV. having students draw conclusions based on the visual

    A. I, II, and III

    B. II, III, and IV

    C. I, II, III, and IV

    D. I, III, and IV

83. Which of the following technological resources are appropriate for instructional purposes?

    I.   e-mailing pen pals

    II. using electronic messaging to contact a contemporary author

    III. e-mail mentoring

    IV. Internet search engines used for research

    A. I, II, and III

    B. II, III, and IV

C.   I, III, and IV

D.   I, II, III, and IV

84. Having students read a biography of a scientist is an example of

A.   integrating the language arts.

B.   emphasizing the importance of science.

C.   teaching students about the genre of biography.

D.   forcing students to learn about the life of a scientist.

85. A group consisting of two to six students, one designated as the leader and one as a scribe, formed to accomplish a task or discuss a topic is called a

A.   discussion group.

B.   cooperative learning group.

C.   sociometric group.

D.   research group.

ESSAY ITEM

Assignment

Write a critical essay analyzing the following excerpt from Ralph Waldo Emerson's *Essays*. Assume that you are writing for an educated audience, and make sure to support your conclusions with evidence from the text. In your essay

- summarize, in your own words, the author's main argument in this passage;

- make a value judgment about the author's reasoning;

- describe the author's method of persuasion and use of rhetorical devices;

- identify the audience for which the author is most likely writing; and

- describe the extent to which the passage is likely to be effective in persuading this audience, and explain why.

Our age is retrospective. It builds the sepulchers of the fathers. It writes biographies, histories, and criticism. The foregoing generations beheld God and nature face to face; we, through their eyes. Why should not we also enjoy an original relation to the universe? Why should not we have a poetry and philosophy of insight and not of tradition, and a religion by revelation to us, and not the history of theirs? Embosomed for a season in nature, whose floods of life stream around and through us, and invite us by the posers they supply, to action proportioned to nature, why should we grope among the dry bones of the past, or put the living generation into masquerade out of its faded wardrobe? The sun shines to-day also. There is more wool and flax in the fields. There are new lands, new men, new thoughts. Let us demand our own works and laws and worship.

Ralph Waldo Emerson, "Nature," 1836

ANSWER KEY—PRACTICE TEST 2

Question	Answer	Competency
1	C	Knowledge of the English Language
2	A	Knowledge of the English Language
3	B	Knowledge of Literature
4	A	Knowledge of Literature
5	D	Knowledge of Literature
6	A	Knowledge of Literature
7	B	Knowledge of Literature
8	B	Knowledge of the English Language
9	A	Knowledge of Literature
10	B	Knowledge of Literature
11	D	Knowledge of the English Language
12	C	Knowledge of Literature
13	A	Knowledge of Literature
14	D	Knowledge of the English Language
15	B	Knowledge of the English Language
16	A	Knowledge of the English Language
17	A	Knowledge of Methods of Integration
18	B	Knowledge of the English Language
19	A	Knowledge of the English Language
20	C	Knowledge of the English Language
21	D	Knowledge of Literature
22	A	Knowledge of Literature
23	C	Knowledge of Methods of Integration
24	C	Knowledge of Literature
25	D	Knowledge of Literature

Question	Answer	Competency
26	A	Knowledge of Literature
27	B	Knowledge of Literature
28	B	Knowledge of the English Language
29	C	Knowledge of Literature
30	A	Knowledge of Literature
31	A	Knowledge of Literature
32	C	Knowledge of Literature
33	B	Knowledge of Writing
34	C	Knowledge of Literature
35	B	Knowledge of the English Language
36	D	Knowledge of the English Language
37	B	Knowledge of the English Language
38	A	Knowledge of Literature
39	C	Knowledge of the English Language
40	D	Knowledge of Writing
41	A	Knowledge of the English Language
42	B	Knowledge of Writing
43	B	Knowledge of the Reading Process to Construct Meaning
44	D	Knowledge of the Reading Process to Construct Meaning
45	C	Knowledge of the English Language
46	C	Knowledge of the English Language
47	B	Knowledge of the English Language
48	A	Knowledge of the English Language
49	C	Knowledge of the English Language
50	D	Knowledge of the Reading Process to Construct Meaning
51	D	Knowledge of the Reading Process to Construct Meaning
52	B	Knowledge of the Reading Process to Construct Meaning
53	A	Knowledge of the Reading Process to Construct Meaning

Question	Answer	Competency
54	C	Knowledge of Writing
55	C	Knowledge of the Reading Process to Construct Meaning
56	D	Knowledge of the Reading Process to Construct Meaning
57	D	Knowledge of the Reading Process to Construct Meaning
58	A	Knowledge of the Reading Process to Construct Meaning
59	D	Knowledge of the Reading Process to Construct Meaning
60	C	Knowledge of Literature
61	A	Knowledge of the English Language
62	D	Knowledge of Literature
63	C	Knowledge of the English Language
64	A	Knowledge of Listening, Viewing, and Speaking
65	C	Knowledge of Writing
66	C	Knowledge of the Reading Process to Construct Meaning
67	C	Knowledge of the Reading Process to Construct Meaning
68	B	Knowledge of the English Language
69	A	Knowledge of the English Language
70	D	Knowledge of the Reading Process to Construct Meaning
71	B	Knowledge of the English Language
72	A	Knowledge of Listening, Viewing, and Speaking
73	B	Knowledge of the Reading Process to Construct Meaning
74	C	Knowledge of Writing
75	C	Knowledge of Writing
76	D	Knowledge of Writing
77	C	Knowledge of Literature
78	B	Knowledge of Listening, Viewing, and Speaking
79	C	Knowledge of Listening, Viewing, and Speaking
80	C	Knowledge of Listening, Viewing, and Speaking
81	D	Knowledge of Listening, Viewing, and Speaking

Question	Answer	Competency
82	C	Knowledge of Listening, Viewing, and Speaking
83	D	Knowledge of Listening, Viewing, and Speaking
84	A	Knowledge of Methods of Integration
85	B	Knowledge of Writing

PRACTICE TEST 2 PROGRESS CHART

Knowledge of the English Language and Methods for Effective Teaching — —/26

1	2	8	11	14	15	16	18	19	20	28	35	36

37	39	41	45	46	47	48	49	61	63	68	69	71

Knowledge of Writing and Methods for Effective Teaching — —/9

33	40	42	54	65	74	75	76	85

Knowledge of the Use of the Reading Process to Construct Meaning from a Wide Range of Selections — —/15

43	44	50	51	52	53	55	56

57	58	59	66	67	70	73

Knowledge of Literature and Methods for Effective Teaching —/24

3	4	5	6	7	9	10	12

13	21	22	24	25	26	27	29

30	31	32	34	38	60	62	77

Knowledge of Listening, Viewing, and Speaking as Methods for Acquiring Critical Literacy —/8

64	72	78	79	80	81	82	83

Knowledge of the Methods for Integration of the Language Arts —/3

17	23	84

Ability to Write Well on a Selection from Poetry or Prose, including Fiction or Nonfiction —essay section

DETAILED EXPLANATIONS FOR PRACTICE TEST 2

1. **C.**

   There is an incorrect verb tense agreement between the past tense *was* ("I was on my way") and the present tense *goes* ("when my tire goes flat"). Because the tire and I were both going to the store at the same time, the action occurring to both of us must agree. Thus, the corrected sentence would say, "I was on my way to the store . . . when the tire went flat."

2. **A.**

   Etymology is the study of a word's origins, including its history and evolution. Etymology offers a fascinating perspective from which to view the living aspects of a language's development and growth.

3. **B.**

   Kafka uses hunger as a metaphor for organized religion and spirituality. Author's note: You may recall that Kafka was born in Prague, and thus his original manuscripts, like many other literary masterpieces, are written in a language other than English (in this case, Czechoslovakian). I've included a second version of the opening paragraph, because it is important for you to remember that variations in translations are also an important element in literary interpretation. When you have a moment, compare the subtle (or not so subtle) variations in the two versions. The second is given below. Consider how these variations might influence your literary interpretation.

   In the last decades interest in hunger artists has declined considerably. Whereas in earlier days there was good money to be earned putting on major productions of this sort under one's own management, nowadays that is totally impossible. Those were different times. Back then the hunger artist captured the attention of the entire city. From day to day while the fasting lasted, participation increased. Everyone wanted to see the hunger artist at least daily. During the final days there were people with subscription tickets who sat all day in front of the small barred cage. And there were even viewing hours at night, their impact heightened by torchlight. On fine days the cage was dragged out into the open air, and then the hunger artist was put on display particularly for the children. While for grown-ups the hunger artist was often merely a joke, something they participated in because it was fashionable, the children looked on amazed, their mouths open, holding each other's hands for safety, as he sat there on scattered straw—spurning a chair—in black tights, looking pale, with his ribs sticking out prominently, sometimes nodding politely, answering questions with a forced smile, even sticking his arm out through the bars to let people feel how emaciated he was, but then completely sinking back into himself, so that he paid no attention to anything, not even to what was so important to him, the striking of the clock, which was the single furnishing in the cage, merely looking out in front of him with his eyes almost shut and now and then sipping from a tiny glass of water to moisten his lips. (Translation by Ian Johnston, Malaspina University-College, Nanaimo, British Columbia, Canada, *www.mala.bc.ca/~Johnstoi/kafka/hungerartist.htm*)

4. **A.**

   Grown-ups view him as a joke. While the text supports this conclusion, substantiating evidence can be found in the instructor's guide that accompanies the seventh edition of the *Norton Introduction to Literature*: "Less obvious . . . is the idea that the hunger artist represents a religious figure of some sort or, in slightly different terms, the spiritual side of humankind, the soul."

5. **D.**

   Geoffrey Chaucer used this poetic style in the *Canterbury Tales* and *The Legend of Good Women*.

6. **A.**

   A sonnet is a lyric poem consisting of a single stanza of 14 lines of iambic pentameter linked by an intricate rhyme scheme.

7. **B.**

   A soliloquy is a monologue in which a character speaks his or her thoughts and feelings aloud.

8. **B.**

   A metaphor is an example of figurative language.

9. **A.**

   T. S. Eliot's *The Waste Land* is a poetic example of modernism.

10. **B.**

    In an imperfect or slant rhyme scheme, corresponding vowel sounds are only approximate, and sometimes the rhymed consonants are similar rather than identical.

11. **D.**

    Syntax is the order and arrangement of words or symbols forming a logical sentence. It is not a study of words (B), nor does it study synonyms (A).

12. **C.**

    An allusion makes reference to a well-known piece of literature, mythology, religion, or history.

13. **A.**

    The Bluest Eye, by Toni Morrison, tells a story of growing up as a black child wishing to have blue eyes. Reading this book might promote a student's ability to relate to others who wish to be something they are not.

14. **D.**

    A morpheme is the smallest unit that a word can be broken into. *Pin,* for example, cannot be broken into a smaller form and still have meaning.

15. **B.**

    Affixes are also known as bound morphemes because they attach to a root or stem morpheme. A prefix, such as *–un*, attaches to the beginning of a word, whereas a suffix, such as *–ing,* attaches to the end of a word.

16. **A.**

    A metaphor is a figure of speech containing an implied comparison in which a word or phrase ordinarily and primarily used for one thing is applied to another for thematic, dramatic, or other type of effect, as in "All the world's a stage, and we are merely players."

17. **A.**

Interdisciplinary activities involve several subject areas and include reading, technology, math, and writing.

18. **B.**

One of the most misunderstood and misused punctuation marks, the colon tells the reader that what follows is closely related to the preceding clause, as in "A dedicated artist requires four things: brushes, paint, canvas, and an eye for beauty."

19. **A.**

A verbal phrase that does not refer to a specific noun or noun phrase is known as a dangling modifier.

20. **C.**

In the sentence "Last night I shot an elephant in my pajamas," the prepositional phrase "in my pajamas" is meant to modify the subject, *I,* not the object, *elephant.* Including the information in a new clause—"while I was wearing my pajamas"— makes the sentence's meaning clear.

21. **D.**

Because some learning skills can be dependent on the environment (e.g., a student might be able to calculate math problems in a classroom environment under controlled conditions but not outside of the classroom), to successfully assess literary skills, the teacher must watch students perform in authentic, rather than controlled, environments.

22. **A.**

To present an oversimplification of the plot and thematic summary of any literary work is to do the reader a disservice as it can lead to misinterpretation of the work as a whole.

23. **C.**

An integrated lesson involves more subject areas and therefore consists of more areas to assess than a nonintegrated lesson.

24. **C.**

Literary naturalism is the belief that every person exists entirely in the order of nature and does not have a soul or any participation in a religious or spiritual world beyond nature. Staged in an indifferent, deterministic universe, naturalistic texts "often describe the futile attempts of human beings to exercise free will in a universe that reveals free will as an illusion."

25. **D.**

There are strong ideological differences between W. E. B. Du Bois's *The Souls of Black Folk* (1902) and Booker T. Washington's *Up from Slavery* (1901). The two texts established lasting battle lines on major issues dealing with racial identity and civil rights in the United States.

26. **A.**

An epic poem is an extended narrative poem based on the heroic exploits and/or extraordinary adventures of an individual involved in an extended quest. The hero is usually a male character who is capable of superhuman feats and performs in a way that reflects and lauds the central beliefs and culture of his society.

27. **B.**

Used in various forms of English poetry, including blank verse, sonnets, and heroic couplets, iambic pentameter is five feet per line of one light syllable followed by a stressed syllable. (A foot is a unit of poetic meter composed of syllables arranged in a pattern of accented and unaccented syllables.)

28. **B.**

Alliteration is the repetition of a consonant sound occurring at the beginning of a word or of a stressed syllable within a word, as in "Peter Piper picked a peck of pickled peppers" or "She sells seashells down by the seashore."

29. **C.**

Concrete or pattern poems use visual shapes to present their content, such as a poem about a goblet written in the shape of a drinking glass, or George Herbert's "Easter Wings" and "The Altar."

30. **A.**

Both English and Italian sonnet structures require the heroic couplet (lines of iambic pentameter that rhyme in pairs: *aa, bb, cc,* etc.) to appear at the end of the stanza.

31. **A.**

The sonnet is saturated with metaphors of nature from "summer days" to flower "buds" in "May," intertwined with images of life and death. As the presumably male narrator extends his contemplations, he realizes that as long as people live, see, and breathe, his affection will too.

32. **C.**

Gothic novels, such as Horace Walpole's *The Castle of Otronto* (1764), emerged in the later part of the eighteenth century and are still a popular form of literary entertainment today.

33. **B.**

A working thesis, as opposed to a finished or final thesis, is a general idea of the direction your essay will take but one that will ultimately be refined and clarified as your essay develops.

34. **C.**

The Pre-Raphaelites were a group of poets who attempted to return to the ideals of truthfulness, simplicity, and art that existed before the Italian Renaissance.

35. **B.**

A mother tongue is a person's indigenous or native language—that is, the first language he or she learns to speak.

36. **D.**

An adverb is a word that modifies a verb, an adjective, or another adverb. In the sentence "Pull gently on an old rope," the adverb *gently* modifies the verb *pull*.

37. **B.**

A complete sentence must have a noun and a verb.

38. **A.**

   The graveyard poets were a group of eighteenth-century poets—Thomas Gray, Edward Young, and Thomas Parnell—who wrote meditative poems usually set and/or written in a cemetery, contemplating the happenstances of life and death.

39. **C.**

   A paragraph is a group of sentences that develop one main idea.

40. **D.**

   Verb tense indicates the relationship between the action and the time the action takes or took place, as in "I swam earlier this morning" (past tense), "I am swimming now" (present tense), and "I will swim tonight" (future tense).

41. **A.**

   As stated earlier, an adverb modifies a verb, adjective, or another adverb.

42. **B.**

   Paraphrasing is restating a text or thesis in your own words, thereby making the idea or topic clearer to understand for both the writer and the reader.

43. **B.**

   Increasing the amount of time the student spends on repetition and review is an effective way to help a student with reading retention problems. Generally speaking, lesson plans should include more time for repetition and review than most people consider necessary.

44. **D.**

   The long-term assessment study found that at the ages of 9, 13, and 17, "children with parents who had some education after high school had the highest reading scores."

45. **C.**

   A homophone or homonym is a word that is pronounced the same way as another word but has a different meaning and/or spelling, as in *two, to,* and *too.*

46. **C.**

Onomatopoeia nouns are words that imitate or mimic the sound they represent, as in *buzz, hiss, whoosh,* and *ding-dong*.

47. **B.**

A dangling modifier is a word or phrase that modifies a word not clearly stated in the sentence. A modifier describes, clarifies, or gives more detail about a concept, and should appear next to the words or idea it modifies. The dangling modifier in answer choice (B) is the prepositional phrase "After completing the course on grammar," which should modify *Ian* but instead is modifying *Ian's essays*. A corrected sentence is "After completing the course on grammar, Ian wrote essays that showed great improvement."

48. **A.**

Morphology is the study of the fundamental structure and formation of words, including inflection, derivation, and the formation of compound words.

49. **C.**

Although English is a compilation of many languages, it originates primarily from German.

50. **D.**

Many of the classic stories for children exist in the realm of fantasy because of the timeless quality of such tales. Fantasy allows children to explore places and events that have never taken place, and will never take place, yet somehow contain messages that we can discuss, savor, and learn from. Faith Ringgold, an author of books for children, has stated, "One of the things you can do so well with children is to blend fantasy and reality. Kids are ready for it; they don't have to have everything lined up and real. It's not that they don't know it's not real, they just don't care."

51. **D.**

If you have ever read any stories that begin with a spoiled princess, you know that characters like Bessie typically undergo some kind of fantastic change.

52. **B.**

    Bessie's transformation is typical of books with a princess theme. Some examples are *The Paper Bag Princess*, by Robert Munsch; *The Frog Prince, Continued*, by Jon Scieszka; *Princess Furball*, by Charlotte Huch; and *Sleeping Ugly*, by Jane Yolen.

53. **A.**

    A K-W-L isn't just for content area lessons. *K* stands for "Know" and suggests activating students' prior knowledge by asking what they already know. *W* indicates what the students "Want" to know, and *L* stands for discussing what the students "Learned" after reading the passage. Some youngsters come to think of fairy tales as "babyish" or "girlish." A K-W-L discussion, laced with stories read aloud, helps children to recognize how delightful and charming this genre can be and helps them to figure out the rules of the genre, which improves their reading and writing.

54. **C.**

    This is the next step in the writing process.

55. **C.**

    Miscue analysis is designed to assess the strategies that children use in their reading. Goodman was interested in the processes occurring during reading, and he believed that any departure from the written text could provide a picture of the underlying cognitive processes. Readers' miscues include substitutions of the written word with another, additions, omissions, and alterations to the word sequence.

56. **D.**

    Comprehension is shown when the reader questions his or her intent for reading. For example, students might be reading a story to find out what terrible things befall the main character. The rationale for choosing a book might be an interesting bit of information (A), but it is not a major topic of discussion with students. Sharing personal information (B) creates a certain bond, but that is not directly relevant to the question. It is also important that all students are on task before the beginning of a lesson (C), but that is a smaller part of the skill modeled in answer choice (D).

57. **D.**

   The library offers students books, articles, journals, and other materials that can help them to do research. The Internet is a very useful tool because of its convenience and its access to many sites. Interviews with relevant people can offer an important glimpse into the "personal" stories or issues of a topic.

58. **A.**

   Editorializing is giving an opinion about an occurrence or an issue. Answer choices (B) and (C) are factual statements. Choice (D) is a straightforward question. The use of *well-deserved* in answer choice (A) illustrates editorializing because it gives the writer's opinion about the applause.

59. **D.**

   A fable is a story that teaches a lesson; therefore, the passage can be classified as a fable. A narrative is generally a long fictional piece. A character analysis scrutinizes one or more characters that are presented. An editorial gives an opinion on a specific subject.

60. **C.**

   A limerick is a humorous poem in the rhythm *a-a-b-b-a*. The first two lines rhyme; the second two lines rhyme; and the last line rhymes with the first two lines. An elegy (A) is a mournful poem. A ballad (B) is a long poem that tells a story. Haiku (D) is a form of poetry with a 17-syllable verse, divided into three units of 5, 7, and 5 syllables, respectively.

61. **A.**

   Alliteration is the repetition of consonant sounds. Onomatopoeia (B) occurs when a word actually sounds like the sound it makes. Imagery (C) is a way to portray something by comparison. Symbolism (D) occurs when a word or phrase represents something else.

62. **D.**

   Illustrating the poem would allow younger children to visualize its humor, while clapping their hands as the poem is read reinforces its rhythm. Older children could write their own poems in this style.

63. **C.**

A metaphor is a comparison between two items without the use of *like* or *as*. In the proverb, death is called a black camel. A simile (B) is a comparison that uses *like* or *as*. Alliteration (A) is the repetition of a consonant sound, and hyperbole (D) is an exaggeration.

64. **A.**

The statement tries to influence readers by telling them that all their friends own this particular item. This device is known as climbing on the bandwagon. A testimonial (B) is a quote by someone, whether by name or anonymous, that vouches for the product. Card stacking (C) is the intentional organization and arrangement of material to make one position look good and another position look bad. A glittering generality (D) is use of an emotionally appealing word or concept to gain approval without thinking.

65. **C.**

This method, known as Call-Up, is a note-taking strategy. Answer choices (B) and (D) are incidental skills that are being taught by this strategy in which the focus is taking organized notes. However, organizational skills are the primary strategy that is being taught by this approach. Choice (A) is incorrect because the assignment described in the question is not creative writing but writing to learn and interpret information.

66. **C.**

The lines are spoken by Juliet in *Romeo and Juliet*, by William Shakespeare.

67. **C.**

Historical almanacs contain yearly data of certain events, including the times for sunrise and sunset and weather-related data and statistics, so answer choice (C) is correct. Historical atlases contain a collection of historical maps. These maps may or may not include population data, so answer choice (A) is incorrect. Historical population data may best be found in government publications on the census. An encyclopedia article would contain a factual summary of the colonial period and the American Revolution but may not include an analysis of the role of Fort Mackinac during the American Revolution because encyclopedias attempt to give overviews rather than interpretations or analysis; therefore, choice (B) is incorrect. A secondary source on Michigan during the colonial period might better address the topic. Information on when the first treaty was signed and the terms of the treaty would most likely appear in a history book or government publication. A participant's diary may not be as accurate, thus (D) is not the correct answer choice.

68. **B.**

    Presence of *the* before *Westtown's* means that the reference is to the council, not to a council belonging to Westtown. The other answer choices are all currently correct, and changing them would make them nonstandard.

69. **A.**

    The editorial is suggesting that the population loss is a bad thing and that proposed changes would be a good thing. Because population loss is something the author wants stopped, or at least lessened, *alleviate*, which means to lessen, is the only possible answer.

70. **D.**

    The subject of the first clause is *each*, which is singular, so the verb should be *has*.

71. **B.**

    Answer choice (A) is wrong because it makes no sense within the sentence; the zoning regulations cannot be easy to change. Choice (C) makes sense, but its use of *them* is ambiguous: does it refer to the authors or the regulations? Answer choice (D) is wrong because, if the authors said the regulations would be hard to change, the word *apparently* earlier in the sentence would make no sense. Thus, choice (B) is the best answer.

72. **A.**

    Writers trying to persuade their readers can base their arguments on facts, character, or emotions.

73. **B.**

    An anecdotal record is an account of an incident written as soon as possible after the incident occurred.

74. **C.**

    A supportive classroom environment for writing should consist of a community of writers, have scheduled writing days and times, use writing portfolios, and include time to share and discuss writing.

75. **C.**

It is not appropriate or useful to respond to student writing by simply saying, "Good work." Students need encouragement and positive reinforcement.

76. **D.**

A teacher who circles all the errors in a student's piece of writing is emphasizing the negative rather than the positive, which will not help students learn.

77. **C.**

Asking students to write their own books is too overwhelming to be a productive writing lesson.

78. **B.**

Both a panel discussion and a debate employ a moderator. In Reader's Theater, students practice reading aloud expressively from a script and then perform for an audience.

79. **C.**

Attentive listening requires children to follow the directions the teacher gives them.

80. **C.**

An ad in which a well-known celebrity endorses a product is termed a testimonial.

81. **D.**

The media's intent is to entertain, persuade, or inform.

82. **C.**

All these strategies are appropriate for assessing a viewing.

83. **D.**

All these technological resources can be used for instructional purposes.

84. **A.**

Reading a biography of a scientist integrates reading and science.

85. **B.**

A cooperative learning group has two to six members, a leader, and a scribe.

ESSAY ITEM

Sample Responses

Seven-Point Response

Emerson's essay makes use of a series of rhetorical questions to develop his thesis that a modern generation does not need to continue the antiquated beliefs of preceding generations into the modern era. Instead, Emerson suggests that "we" develop our own artistic representations, "poetry," "religion by revelation," and "philosophy of insights" based on current issues and viewpoints rather than simply sustaining the obsolete beliefs of previous generations.

Emerson makes a cogent argument by presenting a series of logical, thought-provoking questions aimed at an audience of readers who cannot respond to the speaker directly and must wrestle internally with the answers to the questions he raises.

The writer's thoughts are based on the claim that "our age is retrospective," and there is really no room for the reader to argue against this premise, as there is little argument with the fact that "it writes biographies, histories, and criticism[s]."

Emerson states that our ancestors "beheld God and nature face to face." He asserts that it is not likely that contemporary man will be able to have that same sort of relationship, unless we understand that Emerson, by choosing words such as "God," "sepulchers," and "revelation," is suggesting that modern day intellectuals see beyond the faith-based physical relationship man once enjoyed with "God and nature" and comprehend that these images are metaphors for a modern philosophy of belief and spirit.

This essay achieves its intent of stimulating the intellect and it encourages a modern-day philosophical "revolution," whereby scholars would eliminate outdated "revelations" of earlier generations and embrace the current beliefs of astute thinkers such as Emerson himself.

Five-Point Response

Emerson's *Essay* examines the premise that the social beliefs or values of our ancestors are quite different from those of those living at the start of the nineteenth century. For example, when Emerson suggests that "our age" (the 19th century) "builds the sepulchers of our fathers" (forefathers or ancestors), he is making a two-fold argument, in the form of a double-entendre. First, the author employs the idea that contemporary society erects monuments to ancestors that adorn and celebrate their archaic achievements. Second, Emerson makes reference to "sepulchers" which means "tombs" and places these same "fathers" in a "dead" environment; an environment that is no longer of "philosophical" or pragmatic social utility to a modern generation.

The use of a double-entendre is effective as the foundation of Emerson's argument, which states that while we may need to maintain these familial representations of the past to address the contention that those who do not learn from history are bound to repeat it. At the same time, we still move with the understanding that our modern generation needs to establish its own viable philosophies and artistic artifacts based on current needs, beliefs, and understandings and not those of past generations.

Emerson makes a compelling argument. He presents irrefutable facts since he presents them as rhetorical questions that serve as simple statements of fact disguised in the form of questions, and because they are facts, they are not debatable.

In using this rhetorical question structure, Emerson sets the premise by way of a type of soliloquy that you, as the reader, must accept. If you accept this, you must also accept his logical conclusion based on those facts. It is interesting that Emerson used ancient Aristotelian logic to present his ideas on the need for new ideologies.

Three-Point Response

Emerson makes it clear in his essay that he doesn't think one generation can learn from an earlier one. He thinks the ideas of previous generations are out of date, and useless. He seems to be suggesting that there is no point in accepting the "philosophies and insights" of our ancestors.

But clearly Emerson is wrong because it is obvious that we can learn a lot from our "fathers." In the Bible, for example, we are told that "our fathers" talked to "God, face to face," so how or why would we question this direct authority? Since, according to Emerson, we don't talk to God directly anymore, how is this modern day "revelation" to come from? Because not answering the questions that he asked, Emerson provides his reader with "dry bones of the past" meaning that our ancestors have nothing worthwhile to offer a modern thinker.

Emerson is trying to get us to "demand our own works and laws and worship," but doesn't tell us what is wrong with the old ways. To some, including Emerson, just the fact that they are old is reason enough to replace them. To others, the longevity of these ways is what makes them valuable. By referring to the past as a pile of "dry bones," Emerson lets us know that he finds them worthless, but does not acknowledge that the past can also be a source of familiarity and comfort.

Overall, by not addressing the possible answers to the questions he raises, Emerson is trying to persuade his reader by force rather than by a point/counterpoint argument.

One-Point Response

Emerson's *Nature* essay seems to me to be more about religion than it is about Nature. I mean Sunshine, streams, and floods are parts of nature but I don't really see what they have to do with God and worship and all. Unless he means that God made the floods and the fields and all. I guess maybe that's what he means when he says he demands his own laws to worship. Why doesn't Emerson just go to another church if he doesn't like the one he's in?

Part of what's so hard to understand is his language that he uses. He uses lots of big words that are hard to understand and they really don't make any sense but they do make the essay really hard and boring to understand. He could just have used regular words to say what he wanted to say and then the whole things would be easier to understand. So for me it was hard to understand what he wanted me to know, and he sounds stupid because no one really talks like that or uses words like that anymore.

I guess he means that maybe like when you have a friend and she gets married outside rather than in a church, like my friend who got married in her aunt's garden last spring, that it's like bringing the church outside into nature and than you can have religion along with nature. Like she had her bouquet made up of all the flowers in her aunt's garden and then the bride's maids dresses were the colors of the flowers in the garden and decorated with the flowers from her actual garden, and the minister wore a flower from her garden on his jacket, so its like Emerson was saying that you can have flowers in church or church in your flowers.

So maybe a "sepulcher" is like a church or a garden or something where they decorate it with lots of flowers and crosses and holy water and people go there to pray. Than they can be praying to god and still smell the flowers and see god's bounty and think about how beautiful the garden is thanks to god. Maybe Emerson is saying then that the gardens and the world is beautiful thanks to God and we should be thankful too to god for the flowers and gardens and our fathers who love us.

DETAILED EXPLANATION OF SCORES ON SAMPLE ESSAYS – PRACTICE TEST 2

Seven-Point Response

This response is well developed and summarizes the author's main argument as required by the task. The writer cites Emerson's thesis in the first sentence of the first paragraph. He then uses several quotations to support this thesis. The next three paragraphs provide in depth thought about the Emerson excerpt. By stating in the second paragraph that Emerson makes a "cogent argument," the writer has made the required value judgment of the author's reasoning. The writer uses numerous quotations to describe the author's method of persuasion. The final paragraph is used by the writer to affirm the effectiveness of the passage by stating that the "essay achieves its intent." He goes on to explain how it does that. The writer's choice of vocabulary is excellent and used correctly. This well written essay is done deserves the highest possible score.

Five-Point Response

This is a fairly well-developed response. While not as insightful as the seven-point response, it does summarize Emerson's thesis in the first paragraph and uses quotations to lay out the points that support that thesis. The writer refers to Emerson's use of double-entendre twice, once in the first paragraph and again at the start of the second paragraph. While the term is used correctly, the use of it twice detracts from its impact. The final paragraph, rather than summarizing the thesis and the supportive arguments presented, discusses the logic of the argument presented. A stronger response would have included a brief summary of the entire essay.

Three-Point Response

In this response, the writer, rather than deal with the premise that Emerson presents, argues against it and actually accuses him of being wrong. The writer seems to jump to conclusions about what Emerson is trying to communicate to his reader without citing the necessary supportive evidence. In the final paragraph, the writer, rather than summarizing what has been said, changes focus completely. He simply accuses Emerson of trying to persuade through the use of force rather than by responding to each argument in a point/counterpoint fashion. A better-written response would have complied with the specifics of the task at hand, summarized the arguments made, and used a stronger, more sophisticated vocabulary to do so.

One-Point Response

This is a naïve interpretation of what Emerson is trying to say. The writer, by his own admission, is guessing at Emerson's intent. In addition, the writer obviously, and again by his own admission, has difficulty understanding the vocabulary that Emerson chose. There are several problems with sentence construction, such as the run-on sentence at the start of paragraph three, and the sentences that are awkwardly constructed, such as the second sentence in paragraph three. The fact that the entire paragraph consists of only two sentences should have alerted the writer to problems, but evidently went unnoticed. In the final paragraph, the writer is guessing at the meaning of "sepulcher," and has guessed wrong. This lack of understanding makes the entire last paragraph irrelevant. Further, there are problems with usage such as "than" instead of "then," and problems with mechanics in that the word *God* should be capitalized in the context in which the writer is using it. The writer failed twice to capitalize it —until the third occasion when he did capitalize the word. Therefore, this response lacks sophisticated, in-depth analysis, proper use of vocabulary, and proper mechanics. It would have received a higher score had not these problems been so rampant.

Index

FTCE English 6–12

Index

NOTES

The Best Teachers' Test Preparation for the

FTCE

Florida Teacher Certification Examinations

General Knowledge

Edited by leading Florida-based specialists in teacher education

Timed Practice Exams with Instant Scoring

REA's Software for the FTCE

- **3 Full-Length Exams** with detailed explanations

- **All Competencies** covered in reviews

- **Test Strategies** for passing the FTCE

Available at your local bookstore or order directly from us by sending in coupon below.

Installing REA's TESTware®

SYSTEM REQUIREMENTS

Pentium 75 MHz (300 MHz recommended) or a higher or compatible processor; Microsoft Windows 98 or later; 64 MB available RAM; Internet Explorer 5.5 or higher.

INSTALLATION

1. Insert the FTCE English 6-12 CD-ROM into the CD-ROM drive.

2. If the installation doesn't begin automatically, from the Start Menu choose the RUN command. When the RUN dialog box appears, type d:\setup (where d is the letter of your CD-ROM drive) at the prompt and click OK.

3. The installation process will begin. A dialog box proposing the directory "C:\Program Files\REA\FTCE_English612\" will appear. If the name and location are suitable, click OK. If you wish to specify a different name or location, type it in and click OK.

4. Start the FTCE English 6-12 TESTware® application by double-clicking on the icon.

REA's FTCE English 6-12 TESTware® is **EASY** to **LEARN AND USE**. To achieve maximum benefits, we recommend that you take a few minutes to go through the on-screen tutorial on your computer. The "screen buttons" are also explained here to familiarize you with the program.

TECHNICAL SUPPORT

REA's TESTware® is backed by customer and technical support. For questions about **installation or operation of your software**, contact us at:

Research & Education Association
Phone: (732) 819-8880 (9 a.m. to 5 p.m. ET, Monday–Friday)
Fax: (732) 819-8808
Website: www.rea.com
E-mail: info@rea.com

Note to Windows XP Users: In order for the TESTware® to function properly, please install and run the application under the same computer administrator-level user account. Installing the TESTware® as one user and running it as another could cause file-access path conflicts.